How To Use T'

(AS A FIGHTIN

COPYRIGHT c. 1985 by MOON-TA-GU BOOK CO.

All rights reserved. No part of this book may be reproduced or transmitted in any form or by any means, electronic or mechanical, including photocopying, recording or by any information retrieval system, without the written permission of the publisher except where permitted by law. Or for the purpose of review in magazines or newspapers etc.

PUBLISHED BY
MOON TA-GU BOOKS
P/O BOX 792
MURWILLUMBAH NSW 2484 AUSTRALIA

AUSTRALIAN NATIONAL LIBRARY CATALOGUE

I.S.B.N.

0-949132-05-5
AUTHOR

ERLE MONTAIGUE

REPRINTED October 1990

DISTRIBUTED

IN THE U.S.A.

WAYFARER PUBLICATIONS

P/O BOX 26156

LOS ANGELES CA 90026

U.S.A.

Wayfarer Publications also publish the T'AI CHI NEWSLETTER BI-MONTHLY. For subscription rates etc. write to Wayfarer. This Newsletter/Magazine contains articles and comments from the world's leading t'ai chi experts. Wayfarer also have the largest distribution of other books on t'ai chi. CONTACT: MARVIN SMALHEISER:

DISTRIBUTED IN EUROPE BY:

AIRLIFT BOOK Co.
26-28 EDEN GROVE LONDON N7 8EF

PRINTED BY

THE PRINT SPOT

MAIN ST MURWILLUMBAH NSW 2484

AUSTRALIA

Foreword By Dan Inosanto

It gives me great pleasure to write the foreword for Erle Montaigue's book "HOW TO USE T'AI CHI (as a fighting art)".

This book should be of great interest to both t'ai chi practitioners and non-T'ai chi practitioners alike.
A book on T'ai Chi as a "fighting art" is long overdue. There are many people who still recognize and consider T'ai Chi as only a health exercise.

I feel that this book will be very informative to the martial arts community and a must for everyone's martial arts library.

BY DAN INOSANTO

26th November 1985

Dan Inosanto is one of the world's foremost and well known Martial Artists and teaches at 4051 Glencoe Ave, Unit 12. MARINA DEL REY CA 90292 U.S.A. (author).

Books By Dan Inosanto

JEET KUNE DO
THE ART AND PHILOSOPHY OF BRUCE LEE

A GUIDE TO MARTIAL ARTS TRAINING WITH EQUIPMENT VOL. 1

THE FILIPINO MARTIAL ARTS
AS TAUGHT BY DAN INOSANTO

JEET KUNE DO VOL. 2

POSTERTECHNIQUES
JEET KUNE DO NO. 1
JEET KUNE DO NO. 2
ESCRIMA NO. 1
ESCRIMA NO. 2

ALL OF THE ABOVE BOOKS AND POSTERS PUBLISHED BY
KNOW NOW PUBLISHING CO.
3239 So. HILL ST LOS ANGELES CA. 90037 U.S.A.

CHAPTERS

INTRODUCTION   p. 1

CHAPTER 1   The Postures And Their Meaning   p. 8

CHAPTER 2   Punching And Kicking   p. 62

CHAPTER 3   Sparring and Sensitivity Training p. 84

CHAPTER 4   The Classics   p. 95

CHAPTER 5   Long Har Ch'uan   p. 98

CHAPTER 6   Some Other Fighting Techniques   p. 105

CHAPTER 7   Pa-Kua Chang   p. 113

T'AI CHI
COMBAT AND HEALING

The Magazine of The World Taiji Boxing Association with articles and views from many of the world's leading masters of T'ai Chi Ch'uan, Pa-Kua Chang and H'sin-I past and present.

By subscription from
"TAIJI PUBLICATIONS"
P/O Box 792
Murwillumbah NSW 2484
Australia

Erle Montaigue is the Editor of this fine no nonsense Magazine which is sold to over 22 countries.

The subscription rate is:

$20.00 per year in Australia

$25.00 per year in New Zealand

$25.00 U.S. dollars in the USA

£15.00 British Pounds in Europe

The subscription covers mail in Australia and air mail to overseas countries.

VIDEOS

No.1 This teaches the Original Yang Cheng-Fu Form plus basic Qigong.
No.2 This teaches the Original Old Yang Style of Yang Lu-Ch'an
No.3 This teaches the Original Pauchui fighting form plus both small and large san-sau
No.4 This teaches the Original Pa-Kua Chang, both classical circular and linear fighting form and applications
No.5 This teaches the basic pushing hands, all aspects including push feet
No.6 This is a Chinese Masters demo tape including taiji, pa-kua and h'sin-I
No.7 Advanced techniques of Taiji and Pa-kua
No.8 Internal Weapons, double knife (small sword), taiji short stick and pa-kua staff. Plus sparring.
No.9 Tung's Fast Form. Invented by Tung Ying-Chieh
No.10 Qigong Basics. Breathing with stances
No.11 How To Use Taiji And Pa-Kua for Fighting, adjunct to this book
No.12 Knife And Stick Fighting the Taiji way
No.13 Chen Style with Yuan Han-Yong From Shanghai
No.14 Arnis
No.15 Combat Wrestling And Dim-Mak Point Striking
No.16 Advanced Qigong Principles And Practise
No.17 Chinese Masters Demonstrate
No.18 Montaigue Workshop Modules
No.19 Montaigue Workshop Modules
No.20 Advanced Push Hands
No.21 Taiji Secrets. What the Masters don't tell you! Plus Dim-Mak applications from both taiji forms.

NB/. As of this date, we only have Nos. 3,15,16,20 and 21 in the NTSC system for the USA. No.21 is in two parts for the USA because of it's length.

Write To Moon Ta-Gu Books For A Free more comprehensive cattledog.

ABOUT THE AUTHOR

Erle Montaigue received the degree of MASTER from China in May 1985 when he and eight others became the first Westerners to perform at the China National Wushu Championships in that year. The Vice Chairman of the China Wushu Committee Master Wang Xin-Wu presented Erle with his degree upon his completion of the 1985 tour.
Master Chu King-Hung
Erle started his t'ai chi training in 1968 in Australia and in 1973 shifted to London where he became one of the first students of Master Chu King-Hung. Chu is one of three disciples of the late Yang Sau-Chung the son of Yang Ching-Fu and Great granson of the founder of the Yang Style, Yang Lo-Sim (Lu-Chen).
Erle Montaigue has been a professional wrestler and this sometimes shows in his unorthodox training methods. He believes that people must find their own path in t'ai chi and not spend too much time with their teacher. Only long enough to receive the basics. Erle learnt the basic foundation from Master Chu and various other teachers from around the world, then he worked on the basics until he has now come about to his own way of training and teaching, although he still teaches the basics as they were taught to him. The advanced fighting techniques however are his own, with a little help from anyone that he could beg borrow or steal the good information from.

Master Erle Montaigue believes in taking as much information as you can from as many different sources and then working it out for yourself. This is the only way to become your own master and not someone else's disciple.

Erle has been given the task of course co-ordinator for the NATIONAL COACHING ACCREDITATION SCHEME FOR KUNG-FU in Australia for the T'ai Chi and PaKua part of this scheme. His books are sold around the world including China. He is the Kung-Fu Journalist for the Magazine Australasian Fighting Arts and his many articles have helped to make t'ai chi the recognised great martial art that it was intended to be.
Erle has his own school in Sydney Australia.

INTRODUCTION

HOW TO USE T'AI CHI

(AS A FIGHTING ART)

By Erle Montaigue

For any martial art to stay great there must be some element of change built into it's structure so that it is able to change as the general standard of fighting changes and improves. All of the great classical martial arts were founded in an era when all martial arts were still evolving and people simply used different methods of attack and defence, methods that were still very basic. The foundation of all the classical martial arts were based upon the practise of certain forms or katas which themselves were based upon the methods of attack and defence of the time. T'ai chi is one of these great classical martial arts and as such is also based upon these rules. Any founders of a martial art who had some insight into the changing nature of martial arts would build into their art some element where-by the practitioner was still able to use the art in year to come and not be bogged down by classical manouvers no longer relevant to the time.

The Classical school of Chinese Kung-Fu, T'ai Chi Ch'uan has such an element of change built into it. These training methods are relatively unknown due to the fact that most people practise t'ai chi nowadays to gain the great healing benefits that this art has to offer, so when someone wishes to learn a little more, ie; how to use t'ai chi to defend oneself from external attack, all we are able to find out is how to use each of the postures from the classical form in it's fighting sense. The form from any t'ai chi style was not invented so that people could learn how to fight. It was invented to give us some of the pre-requisites of any great martial art, good health in mind and body; co-ordination of mind and body; perfect timing; perfect balance; relaxation and sub-conscious reaction.

If we take the classical forms from t'ai chi and attempt to use them in a fighting sense, they will probably work against someone who is not a trained fighter, (unexperienced street fighters included) provided that we have practised for long enough. But take these classical techniques and pit them against a modern day trained fighter and we see a different story. Fighters just don't attack as they used to 400 years ago. We no longer use large open stances in order to gain more power, we use centrifugal force with more normal western boxing stances to gain power. We no longer attack and then leave the attacking portion there for someone to grab, we use whipping types of attacks which are very fast, full of power and get the fist or foot in and out with great speed not giving enough time for someone to use a grappling technique. What we are not taught in our t'ai chi training are the most advanced technqiues of "Technique to gain no technique."

FORM:
THE FOUNDATION OF T'AI CHI CH'UAN

Without form we would not have t'ai chi or indeed any of the classical martial arts. The forms give us the basics which are essential for eventually using t'ai chi as a fighting art. Many people ask me why I insist on teaching t'ai chi as a martial art when all most of them want out of it are the great healing benefits.

There are two ways that we are able to practise t'ai chi. We can take it for it's exercise value where-by the practitioner uses only the movements to gain some health benefits, or we can take it a step further into a ch'i or energy level in order to gain much greater healing benefits. This is the area where t'ai chi has become so famous for it's healing properties. Using t'ai chi as an exercise only, we only gain a little exrcise as most people doing it for this reason would never venture beyond the slow form. Doing it for the other reasons, we are able to cure disease and cause every internal and external organ in the body to become strong as well as gain mind/body co-ordination. It is written of t'ai chi that it can help to cure most diseases. One of my students came to me with what he thought was arthritis in his ankle. This was so bad that he couldn't walk properly. After some time of practising t'ai chi the pain became worse and so he had an xray taken which showed that nothing was wrong. After some more time had passed and the pain was still there he decided to have another xray taken and this time it showed that new bone was growing where he had had an accident many year before and knocked out some bone in his ankle. This, according to modern medicine is impossible. Now, the foot is almost back to normal.

This sort of healing will not happen if we only practise t'ai chi for exercise. We must <u>know</u> what we are doing in order for the mind to send ch'i to all parts of the body via the acupuncture meridians.

If one imagines that the body is performing some sort of work then the ch'i or internal energy will travel to that portion of the body where the work is being done. However, if the body or any part along the path is greatly tensed then the ch'i is blocked and only a small amount is able to pass. By performing the slow movements of t'ai chi in the correct way, relaxed, calm with no tension etc, and we imagine that we are performing certain martial arts techniques the ch'i will be sent by the mind to the part that is performing the technique. Because we aren't really doing any work as imagined, the ch'i is sort of fooled into moving into those areas and there-by healing organs on the way. This is why we must know the use of each posture in the slow form, not so much for it's fighting value but because of it's healing value. The form also teaches us perfect posture, a pre-requisite for gaining the maximum amount of power for the least possible amount of work. It also teaches us to remain calm in any situation, important for any fighting art.

In a real fighting situation we have no time to think about what technique that we will use and so we must have a means of obtaining a sub-conscious reaction while still using perfect technique. Usually, if the form postures have become sub-conscious one will only use a small part of any particular posture in order to defend against a particular attack, very rarely is the whole technique used as there just isn't enough time.

There are two ways that we are able to learn about 'no technique'. The first is to simply practise the postures so much that they are forced to become sub-conscious. Doing it this way takes quite a long time. If we use the little known technique or training method of 'Long Har Ch'uan' (Dragon Prawn Boxing) it enables us to learn about sub-conscious reaction in a relatively shorter time while still using all of the important basic principles of t'ai chi. (See "General Principles Of T'ai Chi" by Erle Montaigue). We must never skip over the basics of; Form, Push Hands, DaLu and SanSau in order to get there quicker as this will end in failure to gain the highest level of boxing skills that t'ai chi has to offer. Without the basics t'ai chi is just another external style of kung-fu.

LONG HAR CH'UAN

Long Har Ch'uan means 'Dragon Prawn Boxing'. The reason for this is that we use the two arms as 'feelers' with the body slightly concave. The theory is that if someone strikes with a fist, you go in at the waist which causes the attacker to have to reach further to strike, where-as you are able to re-attack at a closer range. See PHOTO No. 1.

Long Har Ch'uan is only a training method which is used in order to gain a certain way of doing things. In kung-fu we try not to place the same sort of limitations on ourselves that some of the external styles do by sticking rigidly to what the forms or katas dictate. We use the forms only as guides to teach us something and then translate what they have taught us into our own particular body types or 'preference.'

Photo No. 1

This preference is quite important as everyone has a particular way of doing things and this way comes easier to that person than any other technqiue and so we try to arrange our training techniques around that particular method. In this way the student is able to utilise his/her own natural body method as a martial art. This is what the training method of Long Har Ch'uan is all about, it teaches us to use what we have naturally rather than trying to change us and place un-natural movements onto our bodies. So, it can be seen that any one person will only ever use a certain 'way' of attack and defence while only ever using three or at the most four fighting technqiues and derivations of these. It's much better to train in only a few techniques than many. This also gets back to why one is practising martial arts. Do you do it for good sport within the school or to defend yourself.

In a classroom and training with your friends, you tend to gain a false sense of security in that we know that no-one is really going to hurt us in our sparring matches and so we use many technqiues just for the sake of using them. In one's first real encounter there usually comes a big shock to the martial artist. People in the street just don't fight as they do in the dojo or dawgwan. I once wrote an article titled, "I'd rather fight a trained martial artist than a street wise fighter" and this is quite true, the street fighter doesn't know that you are a martial artist and so he will not be at all wary of your ability. He will come at you with such force and determination that you will wonder what has hit you. And he will come at you from any direction at any time with anything that he can use as a weapon. So many times have I heard "But I'm a black belt! and I went to pieces." I think that one should have some sort of street experience before a black belt is given. The street fighter doesn't have any fighting stance or wait and choose his moment, he just attacks and attacks. If your method of fighting is not truly sub-conscious then you will lose the fight. This of course depends on how street wise your attacker is, it could be that he is just a relatively harmless drunk and in which case would be relatively easy to take care of gently! But don't allow that sort of a win to give you great confidence, go and kick over a row of Hells Angels bikes and then see how you go. Your technique must be 'no technique and totally dependant upon what your attacker does to you. If it's right to spit in his eye then do it, if it's right to use a perfect kick to his knee then do it but let it just happen. Only then will the t'ai chi principle from the classics of 'stick to and not letting go' be adhered to.

THE CLASSICS

The Classics of t'ai chi are a bunch of old sayings from the various masters who tried to put their advanced experience into words. I don't think that it works too well to put experience into words but as far as t'ai chi or pakua is concerned it's all we have to fall back onto.

These classics are on paper in black and white, they are physical, conscious 'things'. If we read them and then try to do what they say we get into trouble because we must think about it. The classics came out of something that the old masters discovered for themselves, sub-consciously. I don't say that you shouldn't read the classics because they are all that we have to go on and give us some sort of goal to reach for. What we should be trying to do is to experience what the masters experienced then we can be assured that the art is truly ours and not someone else's idea that only they are able to appreciate. Don't take the classics too literally, allow your training methods to give you the classics without having to think about them, then as you discover a certain way you will think, "Oh yes, that's what is meant by that part of the classics etc." Don't try to make the classics give you the technique, allow the technique to give you the classics. "Stick to and not letting go" is a famous classical saying from t'ai chi but if we try to do what it says then it becomes a bit silly, we must use a training method to gain this way of doing things so that it is totally natural and mindless. We don't know that we're doing it. The training methods that give us the classics are all of your t'ai chi training methods of form, push-hands,- da- lu, san-sau and in particular, 'Long Har Ch'uan.'

When one starts his/her t'ai chi training there is no need to read the classics because it will be too advanced. All the beginner should be concerned with is learning the movements in a mindful way with every posture in it's correct position. As the student advances in his/her training, certain lessons are learnt. These lessons aren't physical things like where to put your feet and hands etc, but internal lessons that just come from doing it the right way. These internal lessons become a part of one's own body and mind and no words will be able to express what these lessons are as everyone experiences something different. If one practises in this way and doesn't try to theorise too much or become a cosmic person, then all of the great benefits to be gained from t'ai chi will be yours.

THE POSTURES

AND THEIR APPLICATION

_____CHAPTER ONE

The form or kata of t'ai chi is the first real physical method that we learn. Once one is well versed in ch'i-kung, (see "POWER T'AI CHI CH'UAN BOOK ONE" by Erle Montaigue) the form is the foundation of one's training. This form is made up of many different postures all held together by linking movements to make one long flowing movement which is enlikened to a great flowing river.

It has been said of t'ai chi, that unlike some of the 'harder styles' where what you see is what you get, in t'ai chi we only see 10% of what is really going down. If we take for instance the posture called 'push left' from the Old and New Yang styles, we see a posture that really doesn't say much. See Photo No. 2.

If we look at the real meaning of this posture then it's a different story. Photos Nos. 3, 4 & 4A, 5 & 5A & 5B show that this posture really has a martial meaning.

No. 3 is a block to a left round punch and simultaneous attack to the jaw with a right palm. Nos. 4 & 4A. show a 'peng' block being used to stop a right fist followed by an elbow break. Nos. 5, 5A & 5B show a right (or left as the

No. 2

No. 3

No. 4

No. 4A

No. 5

No. 5A   No. 5B

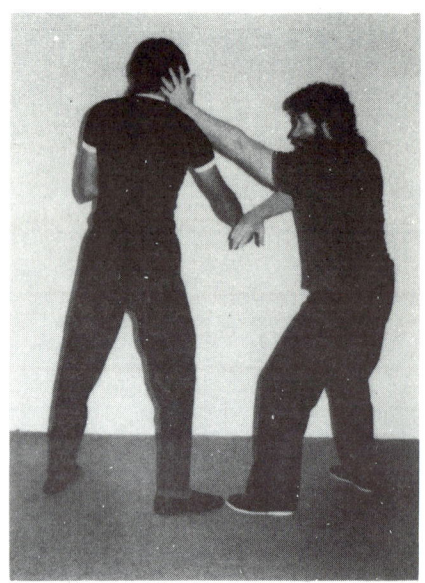

case may be) attack being blocked by left p'eng then the rt. palm almost immediately takes over the block while the left attacks to the face.

  Most of the postures hold this 10% aspect where what we see is no real indication of what we get. Therefore, it can also be said that the t'ai chi form is an abstract way of learning something real. We train the body to perform certain abstract postures so that the sub-conscious mind is able to learn them as fighting postures. If one was to learn the real use of the postures and how they were used, then it would take forever to learn them properly because we are thinking about the martial aspects. If we learn certain abstract movements that only the sub-conscious is able to work out, then we have learnt the use of the postures without even learning them. Then when one is well versed in the slow movements, all that has to be done is to translate the abstract movement into a real form which doesn't take too long.

Learning the slow form in this abstract way also has another meaning. We cause certain internal movements of energy to happen, there-by making our body and mind strong and more in harmony. In the beginning what a student will see and what he/she translates as being representative of that movement will be quite different. There is a gap between what the mind sees and what the body does. As the training progresses, we see a shortening of that gap and eventually the mind and body work as one, a great asset in any martial art.

The abstract form causes healing to take place physically and mentally while internally and sub-consciously we are learning a 'method of fighting. From this form we learn perfect timing. Perfect timing is the singularly most important aspect to have in the martial arts. Timing covers balance, distance, weight and power, yin and yang. But timing must not be saught after, it must just come naturally by practising all of the aspects of t'ai chi.

In learning the real use of the t'ai chi postures, once again they must not be taken as gospel. We must use the postures as a training method so that we are able to use any part of any technique at any time . So when training in the methods given in this book, keep in mind that I am not saying that this is the way that it must be done, you must take what you are able to use naturally and leave the rest. We are given so many techniques in t'ai chi in the hope that we are able to find some techniques that suite us.

You must start out very slowly and precisely at first with the main intention on direction and timing. It's all very well to be able to perform a technique at great speed in the classroom but in a real situation if the power with timing is not there, then the fight is lost. I cannot tell you exactly where to place your limbs in order to derive the greatest amount of power with speed, I can only give you a guideline as everyone is different.

By doing it slowly we are able to find out exactly how to perform the techniques in order to use the least amount of energy for the greatest possible work. At first, break the blocking movement away from the attacking movement in order to learn it correctly. Then as you progress, the block and attack will become as one where-by the block also becomes your attack. Remember that some of these postures are very classical and need to be taken for what they're worth, ie; For the sake of knowing the real meaning and for the health benefits derived from the mind sending ch'i or energy into that area to do work. Some of these techniques are quite good as they are. Some of them will require that you only use a portion of the whole. Just practise them with a partner and chose the ones that suit you the most. It is important to note that although a certain technique may work against your friend in a friendly situation, it must be tested in as realistic a way as possible.

THE POSTURES

PREPARTAION

You are being attacked by either left or right lunge punch to the head. Raise your both arms as in the opening posture of the slow t'ai chi form and block the on-coming arm on either side as you step slightly to one side and forward. See Photo No. 6. Now take another step to behind the attacker and using a squeezing motion from the elbows, pull down onto the shoulder area, (Gall bladder and large intestine meridians) to bring him down backwards. See Photo No. 7. The pull down motion should be a quick jerking motion and not so much a pull backwards. Breathe out and expand the lower abdomen as you attack as you should with all of the attacking motions.

ARN (push) TO THE LEFT

I have already covered 3 of the uses of this posture earlier, there is another. The attacker strikes at your face with a left fist. You block with your right palm as your left palm comes up underneath. Photo No. 8. Next, you attack his face with an open left palm. This is in the case of an attack from the side area. PHOTO No. 49. (p.29)

No. 6

No. 7

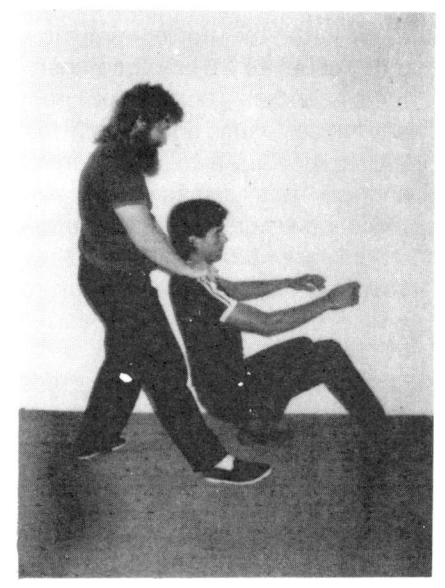

No. 8

No. 9

BLOCK LOW TO THE RIGHT (holding the ball)

This posture is sometimes done in the slow form with the lower arm in the palm up position, this is only done to allow beginners to understand where to place their hands. The correct posture is done with the lower arm in a palm down position. Photo No. 9. In this posture the harder area of the forearm is used to block the attack and so not damage the soft area of the arm. There are times however when the hold the ball posture is used.

You are being attacked with a left low upper punch to your right rib area, (one of the most potent areas to attack). You bring the left arm across to your right as you swivel slightly to the right in order to keep your palms in your centre. Your weight is placed on the left leg to receive the power. You block the attacker's arm from underneath, keeping your right palm on top of your left to stop his hand from slipping upward and re-attacking. Photo No. 10. You must keep your left fingers relaxed to prevent damage. This technique can be practised on both sides one after the other as you swivel on your heels to meet the attack and it can become quite fast. Photo No. 11. This sort of blocking technique can be used to block all kinds of middle area kicks followed up by an immediate attack. (covered in the advanced section.)

P'ENG

P'eng is one of the main techniques in t'ai chi and it's uses are many. I will cover many of the p'eng techniques in the advanced section. It's usual use is that of defence but a more unknown use is that of attack. For p'eng see PHOTO No. 12. If we take up from the last block to the right, we are able to very quickly grab the left wrist with the right palm, quickly step up with your left foot and attack the 'mind point' (in acupuncture, the jaw) with back fist. Phot No. 13.

DOUBLE P'ENG

If your attacker now attacks with right low upper punch to your left rib area, you quickly step back and swivel to your left with the weight on your right foot as you block using the same low block as in photo 11.

PAGE FIFTEEN

No. 10

No. 11

No. 12

No. 13

You then step forward with your right foot and the right fist comes up from underneath your left arm to attack with a downward back fist to the chin. Photo No. 14. Note that the left palm is guarding the attacker's right arm to sense what it will do next. For double p'eng see Photo No. 15.

No. 14   No. 15

PULL DOWNWARD (Lu)
The posture of double p'eng can also be used for the blocking technique to to begin this next posture. You are being attacked by a right (or left) fist. You block using double p'eng with your right arm. Photo No. 16. The left palm now comes over the top of the attacker's wrist

and grabs it with some help from the right palm. Photo No. 17. You then twist the attacker's right wrist in the direction that it does not want to go and pull him downward using the power from the waist. Photo No. 18.

No. 16

No. 17

Be careful with this one when practising as it can cause damage without even trying.

Another use of Lu is is to use it only as a blocking technique. If you are being attacked with left low punch to your right rib area. Swivel to your right to keep your centres in line and slam down onto the opponent's left arm with the back of your left forearm, keeping your right arm underneath to trap the arm. Photo No. 19. If you are being attacked on your left side, swivel to meet it and as

PAGE EIGHTEEN

No. 18   No. 19

you turn, draw both arms in toward you slightly. Then as you meet the attacker's arm, thrust both of your forearms downward to catch his right arm in a scissors block. The power for this comes from the straightening of the left leg. Photo No. 20. If you pull your hands apart you will see that the 'LU' posture is used here.

NB: I will only show photos of those postures that aren't so well known. Most of the major postures are quite well known. For the other postures (ie, what they look like) consult my earlier books or any of the other good books available.)

No. 20   No. 21

CHEE OR (Squeeze, sometimes called press)

From any of the last blocking or attacking movements, bring your left palm to the outside of your right wrist and use lifting energy to attack to his lower stomach area. This attack can either be a powerful pushing movement as in Photo No. 21, or it can be a snapping downward attack upon the abdomen at the junction of the diaphram.

SIT BACK LIKE MONKEY

This posture, Photo No. 22 has three main uses. Firstly, upon receiving a left punch to the right side of your face, you should sit backwards bringing the right foot back and swivel to your right as you block with your 'limp' wrist. Photo No. 23. Almost simultaneously you should bounce forward with your left foot and attack to the jaw with left jab. This should be a snapping punch as it is aimed at the hard boney area. Photo No. 24. This should be

No. 22

No. 23

No. 24

No. 25

done on both sides. The next defencive use of this posture is used against the same attack. Sit back and block as before in photo No. 23. This time you will hook your right palm over the top of his left palm and throw it over to your left side as you swivel to that side changing the weight to your right foot. You will grab his left wrist with your left palm. Photo No. 25. Lifting his left arm up, you step forward and attack the lower left rib area with low centrifugal back fist. Photo No 26. This also should be done on both sides.

The final use of this posture is a break from a strangle grab. Photo No. 27. Follow this with an attacking push to the abdomen. This can be either a snapping attack or a lifting attack. Photo No. 28.

No. 26   No. 27

No. 28 No. 29

SIT BACK LIKE MONKEY (Old Yang Style)

The 'Old Yang Style' or the style as it was before the 20th Century changes had a different use for this posture. Photo No. 29. As a right or left (as the case may be), lower punch is being felt, you should block it on the inside with either forearm. Photo No. 30. Hook your arm under his arm and trap it. Photo No. 31. Now, using the power from your waist, turn to the appropriate side and throw him backwards using your other palm to advantage. Photo No. 32.

SIT BACK READY

Your opponent strikes you to your face with right fist. You should sit backwards and block with your left palm as you strike to his eyes with your right fingers. Photo No. 33. Or, you should grab his left fist with your left palm and use a throw using his elbow as the lever.

PAGE TWENTY THREE

No. 30

No. 31

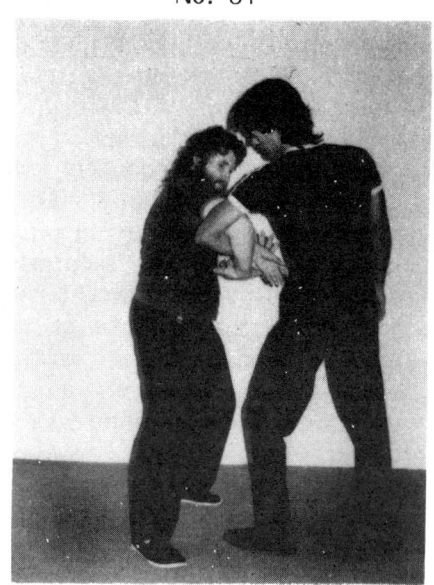

No. 32

No. 33

Photo No. 34. See Photo No. 35 for the posture of 'Sit back ready.'

FISHES IN EIGHT

Your opponent strikes you with right fist at your right side. You should block his arm with your right forearm in a circular fashion, Photo No. 36. Then, simultaneously attack his face with right heel palm as the left palm takes over the block. Photo No. 37.

Another use of this posture is as follows....You are attacked with a punch to the acupuncture (DimMak) points under your left arm. You should block down with your right forearm onto your left forearm to form a scissor block. Photo No. 38. Now swivel to your right and pull the attacker's right palm over to your right. You now strike with your left knife edge palm to his throat as you step forward with your left foot. This is done also on the other side. Photo No. 39.

No. 34   No. 35

PAGE TWENTY FIVE

No. 36

No. 37

No. 38

No. 39

SINGLE WHIP

As your opponent attacks low with a right fist to your lower left rib area, you should block with your right hooked palm and take it over to your right as you swivel to that side, your left fingers point to your right elbow. Photo No. 40. Step forward with your left foot and attack the acupuncture points under his right arm. Your left palm protects you from his re-attack Photo No. 41. This is also practised on the other side and the initial block using hooked palm is used to block upward for head attacks. Continuing the use of single whip: A right fist attacks your face, you should use your hooked right palm to block it over to your right. Photo No. 42. Now attack with left palm to the kidney area. Photo No. 43.

LIFT HANDS

You are attacked by a right or left fist to the upper area. You slap his wrist with your left palm as your right palm slaps his left elbow to break the arm. Your right foot kicks to his knee area. Photo No. 44. You now throw your opponent backwards.

SHOULDER STROKE

You are grabbed onto your right arm and pulled downward. You should go with the momentum and not fight to free your arm. Step in to his chest and use right shoulder to attack his chest. Photo No. 45. Your left palm is there to protect your left elbow from being broken. It should push the left palm away in the case of elbow break. Your right palm protects against knee to your groin.

STORK SPREADS WINGS

There are two uses for this posture, the first is the more commonly known while the second is less known. You are attacked with left fist so you block it outward. You are then attacked with low right fist so you block it downward and kick to his knee. Photo No. 46. OR: You are attacked with left fist to your face. Your right palm blocks it across in a circle to your left as your left pal, comes up underneath to take

No. 40

No. 41

No. 42

No. 43

PAGE TWENTY EIGHT

No. 44

No. 45

No. 46

No. 47

over the block. Photo No. 47. Your left palm looks after the left fist while your right fist circles back up in a centrifugal punch to his left temple. Your left foot kicks to the groin. Photo No. 48. This is one of the most powerful punches in any martial art as it is totally centrifugal.

BRUSH KNEE TWIST STEP

This posture is used to block either a middle straight kick to the stomach or a low punch to the abdomen. If it is the left fist attacking, your left palm will block it over to your left side as you pick up your left foot. Photo No. 50. Or, you can attack with right pounding palm to the chest. Photo No. 51. The palm strike in this posture should not be mistaken for a pushing technique. The palm stays relaxed until impact and then flicks up just upon striking.

No. 48   No. 49

No. 50   No. 51

PLAY THE GUITAR

This has a different action to the lift hands posture although the final positions look the same. As your opponent attacks you with right fist to your head you should block it with your left palm across to your right and a split second later your right palm comes up underneath your left palm to cause the attacking arm to slide. You wil also kick to the knee area with your heel. Your right palm can also punch to the face. Photo No. 52. This is one of the best fighting techniques offered by t'ai chi. It is simple and takes a split second to execute. It is a major part of the advanced 'Long Har Ch'uan' that I will be covering later.

STEP FORWARD, PARRY AND PUNCH

You are being attacked with right fist to your middle area. You should circle your right fist up to your left side and slam it down onto the attacking forearm as you attack to the chest or face with your left palm. Photo No. 53. The attacking fist will probably make use of the downward force cau-

No. 52   No. 53

sed by your right back fist and come back up in a circle to attack to your left face. You will block with your left palm and punch to the heart as you step in. Photo No. 54. A very effective block and simultaneous attack comes from this last punch. As you are being attacked with a left or right straight punch, you block with your left palm in the case of a right attack and immediately punch to the abdomen with your right fist. Photo No. 55.

PULL AWAY AND PUSH

If your opponent grabs your right fist after the last attack you should take your left palm under your right forearm. You then pull your right palm back and sit back, this breaks the hold. (There are of course easier ways to do this,) Photo No. 56. You then use push to the opponent's side. Photo No. 57.

PAGE THIRTY TWO

No. 54

No. 55

No. 56

No. 57

No. 58   No. 59

APPARENT CLOSE UP
If someone tries to attack with choke, you should open both palms underneath his palms, Photo No. 58. Then circle his arms around and push him away. Photo No. 59.

QUICKLY PUNCHING FIST
This posture comes from the Old Yang Style and uses very quick snapping punches and blocks. As you are attacked with left fist (or right), you block very quickly with your right palm in a circular fashion. Photo No. 60. Now you use snap punch to the lower rib area, snapping your fist as it contacts. Photo No. 61. I will be covering the various ways of punching and kicking later.

BACKWARDS LOCKING PALM
This posture also comes from the old Yang Style and is used against a right or left low body punch. As the punch is being felt, the right palm (or left) blocks to your left in a small circle. Photo No. 62. Now your right palm hooks

and traps the arm by making a counter clockwise circle, Photo No. 63. This can then evolve into an arm lock or throw. Photo No. 64.

This is the end of the first 3rd of the form.

No. 60

No. 61

No. 62

No. 63   No. 64

BEGINNING OF 2ND. THIRD

EMBRACE TIGER RETURN TO MOUNTAIN
          This posture is the same in application as 'brush knee twist step'. The difference is that it is performed onto the closed side of the opponent, ie; he attacks from the rear with right fist to your kidney area. You turn and block with your right arm (or left as the case may dictate) Photo No. 65 and attack with palm to his right soft flank. From the classics we are also given another clue as to the use of this posture, "Embrace Tiger Return To Mountain embodies 'pull down and split". This tells us that pull down can also be done from the blocking posture with your right palm grabbing his right wrist and your left palm grabbing his right elbow. Split means to use the elbow as a lever and throw him away using that leverage.

No. 65   No. 66

FIST UNDER ELBOW

From the Classics we read; "This posture protects the middle joint." This is self explanatory. The use of this posture is as follows. You should hammer down onto the forearm of the attacker with your right fist as he attacks with left fist. Then you should attack his face or throat with your left palm. Photo No. 66.

The 'Old Yang Style' has a slightly different application for this posture. As a left face attack is being felt, you should block it with your right forearm. Photo No. 67. Next and almost simultaneously you flick the arm over to your other hand which takes over the block. Photo No. 68. Now you use uppercut to his face, Photo No. 69. This is also performed on the other side and takes about 1/10 th of a second to perform both punches.

STEP BACK AND REPULSE MONKEY

In the new Yang Style this posture is used to block an on-coming lower attack and re-attack to the face or chest using pounding palm. Note that the power for this posture comes from the front leg as it pushes you backwards. <u>Photo 70</u>.

No. 67

No. 68

No. 69

No. 70

TRIPPING REPULSE MONKEY

In the Old Yang Style we have the postures of 'Step Back And Repulse Monkey' which appears in the last third of the form which is the same posture with the same name that appears in the New Yang Style. However, in the second third of the Old Yang Style we have 'Tripping Repulse Monkey' which is different than the more commonly known one.

An attack comes from behind so you turn to block and grab the arm. Photo No. 71. You now place your left (or right as the case may be) foot onto the groin or to the knee of the attacker and throw him forward using the leverage of his arm and your foot in his groin. Photo No. 72.

No. 71   No. 72

PART HORSE'S MANE

You block an attack to your right side using double block, Photo No. 73. You then step in to behind his left foot and attack his axila acupuncture points with your thumb or reverse knife edge palm. Photo No. 74.

PAGE THIRTY NINE

No. 73 No. 74

NEEDLE AT SEA BOTTOM
In the new Yang style this is used to break a hold downward with a jerking thrust. If the opponent is able to hold onto your wrist and pulls backward you should go with the force and turn your right wrist, grabbing his right wrist and poke him under his right arm into his acupuncture points. This is the use of the posture FAN THROUGH BACK. Photo No. 75 For Needle At Sea Bottom see Photo No. 94 on p. 46.

MOVING HANDS LIKE WILLOW TREE
This posture comes from the 'Old Yang Style' and defends against a left punch towards your head or chest. You should block with the 'yang' side of your right forearm. Photo No. 76. Then you attack with back-fist to the head, photo No. 77. You then block a kick downward with both forearms. Photo No.78. Followed by an attack to his face or neck with both palms. Photo No. 79.

PAGE FORTY

No. 75

No. 76

No. 77

No. 78

No. 79   No. 80

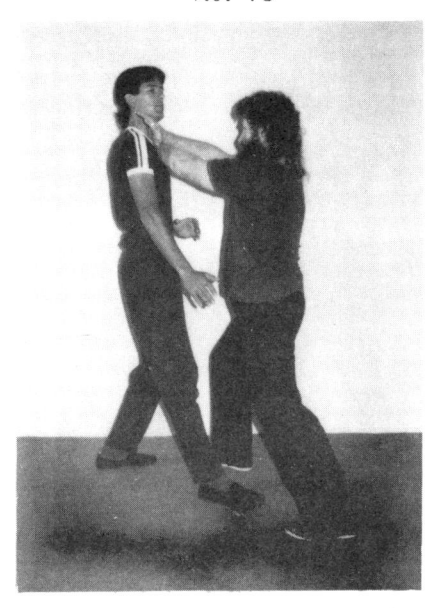

SNAKE COILS AROUND
This posture also comes from the 'Old Yang Style'. Block a left punch with both palms, Photo No. 80. Grab the wrist and use a locking technique to pull him downward, twisting his wrist in the direction that it does not want to go, Photo No. 81. Now use 'Chee' to throw him away, Photo No. 82.

WAVE HANDS LIKE CLOUDS
The classics say of this posture:"Advance three times demonstrating skill with the top of the forearm." This tells us about one of the main uses of this posture, to block attacks to the side using the forearm but there is another use. As a low attack is being felt you should block it downward with your left (or right) palm, Photo No. 83, then in an instant attack with your back-fist. Photo No. 84. This can also be used for a higher attack only you should use an upper block with the rising palm as you attack to the groin with the other.

PAGE FORTY TWO

No. 81

No. 82

No. 83

No. 84

No. 85   No. 86

LIFT HANDS TO HEAVEN
This posture blocks against a front attacking fist, Photo No. 85. If the opponent should follow his natural line of attack he will re-attack with a low punch to your left flank, you should drop your left palm downward to block as you simultaneously attack his face with right palm. This is the posture, HIGH PAT ON HORSE. Photo No. 86.

DRAWING THE BOW
In the 'New Yang Style' you should block a right fist firstly with your left palm as your right palm crosses over, Photo No. 87. Your right palm should now attack to his face. Photo No. 88.

SITTING LIKE A DUCK
This posture comes from the 'Old Yang Style' and blocks a punch from the rear, Photo No. 89. Then you should grab his wrist and using the momentum of your body in sinking downward, twist his wrist in an un-natural way to bring him down, Photo No. 90. If he should pull away and retreat, you should spring up and attack with right toe kick. This is from the

PAGE FORTY FOUR

No. 87

No. 88

No. 89

No. 90

'Old Yang Style.' Photo No. 91.

No. 91   No. 92

SEPARATION OF RIGHT AND LEFT LEGS

Although this posture is not called a kick, it is a kick. Block the opponent's right or left fist with your appropriate palm as you kick to his kidney area or knee. Photo No. 92.

KICK WITH LEFT OR RIGHT HEEL

This is the same action as for the last kick only the heel is used to the soft middle stomach area. This kick is one of the simpler techniques but it requires great technique to be able to use it effectively. The foot has the tendency to slide upward instead of driving inward. Photo No. 93.

NOTE: I will be covering all types of kicking techniques used in t'ai chi in the later chapters of this book. We tend to practise all types of kicking techniques because this is the only way to learn how to defend oneself against them. For instance, we do not necessarily have high roundhouse kicks in t'ai chi but someone who is adept at this sort of kick will use it and we must know how to block such a kick. The usual cop-out for some internalists is that these kicks do not work in the street. I have seen the roundhouse kick used to great advantage in the street because the attackee did not know how to defend against it. Or rather he did know how to defend against it but had received no practise against it. Many kickboxers are able to kick with devastating results. Once one knows the use of the elbow, and I mean <u>know the use</u>, the roundhouse kick can be more damaging to the attacker more-so than the attackee.

NO. 93   No. 94

<u>PUNCH TO GROIN</u>
This is the original posture of the last one and is more useful, although still rather 'exotic'. A kick is being felt to your stomach so you block it with left hook and raise your

No. 95 No. 96

left leg. Photo No. 95. You can now either kick to the opponent's other leg or groin, Photo No. 96, or you can take it through to it's end by lifting his attacking leg up to cause him to fall down onto his back and then attack the groin with punch. Photo No. 97.

TURNING BLOCK WITH DOUBLE LEAPING KICK
Block an attack from the rear or side with your right palm, keeping the left one as a guard. Photo No. 98, kick with snapping instep kick to the axila area with your left foot. Photo No. 99. If the opponent blocks that kick, before the first kick has retreated, leap up and kick with the other foot to anywhere that the foot will reach. Photo No. 100. This posture comes from the 'Old Yang style.' The New Yang Style has a normal right heel kick in this position of the form.

PAGE FORTY EIGHT

No. 97

No. 98

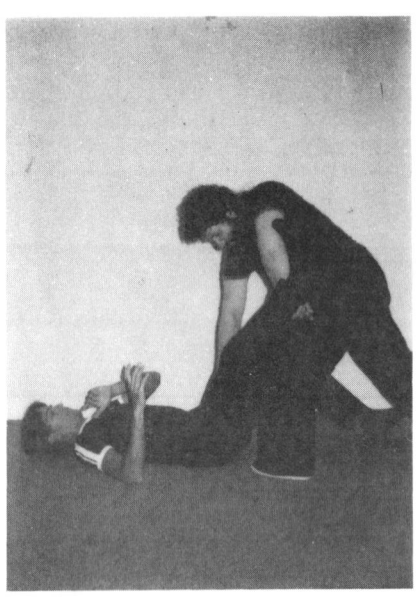

No. 99

No. 100

HIT TIGER LEFT AND RIGHT

From the 'New Yang Style' we have a punch being blocked, Photo No. 101 and a follow up with a feint attack to the head with phoenix punch so that the opponent tries to block that punch, then simultaneously attack to the kidney area with a low punch of the same configuration. Photo No. 102.

No. 101   No. 102

HIT TIGER LEFT AND RIGHT WITH PENETRATION PUNCH

This posture comes from the Old Yang Style and is slightly different than the new Yang.

Block a head punch with upper block, Photo No. 103, the opponent would probably attack low with right fist. You should block it using left hook, Photo No. 104, then immediately attack with snap cross punch. This is 'Hit Tiger.' Photo No. 105. This hook and attack only takes a fraction of a second to perform. If a second attacker comes in from that last posture you might use back fist to his head. Photo No. 106. If he blocks your attack and re-attacks with left fist, you should block it with your right forearm, Photo No. 107, then take over the block with your left palm as you use penetration punch gaining power from a

PAGE FIFTY

No. 103

No. 104

No. 105

No. 106

No. 107   No. 108

twist of your left foot. Photo No. 108. This is performed on both sides.

DOUBLE WIND GOES THROUGH EARS

After using stomach heel kick to his abdomen, the opponent would bend forward. Now, in a fit of over-kill you take his head and slam it down onto your knee, Photo-No.109. Then as he reels backwards you step forward and follow up with double temple punch. Photo No. 110.
This is really a case of over-kill but that's how the form goes.

SIDE KICK

You are being attacked by front kick and you evade by twisting your body and poke to the dim-mak points (acupuncture points) around his heart. Photo No. 111. He would probably block this. You now grab his hand and pull him downward using the momentum of your lowering. Photo No. 112. He would now pull backward so you spring up and attack with side kick to his knee, keeping your palms as guards. Photo No. 113. This is from the 'Old Yang Style.'

No. 109

No. 110

No. 111

No. 112

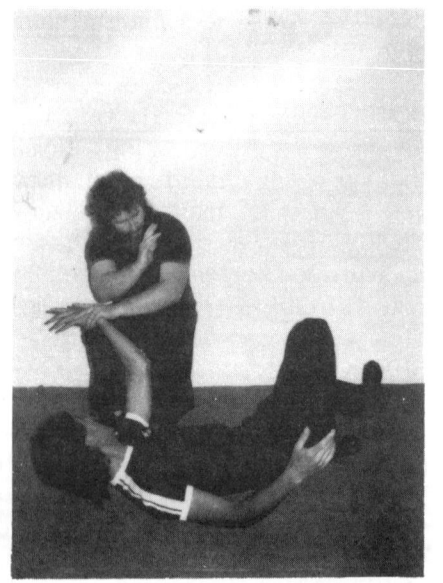

No. 113   No. 115

BLOCK AND USE DOUBLE FINGER JAB

The opponent may attack with double dragon palms (although this is highly unlikely). You should use both palms to block in a circular fashion blocking with the knife edges of both palms. Then you jab with your fingers to his vital points near his abdomen. Photo No. 115. This comes from the 'Old Yang Style.' (Please Note that there is no photo No. 114.

LIFT HANDS

This form of 'lift hands' comes from the 'Old Yang Style'.

Block a right (or left) punch with your right (or left as the situation dictates), Photo No. 116. You now step up with your left foot and using your other palm you break the elbow as shown in Photo No. 117.

No. 116   No. 117

THIS IS THE FINISH OF
THE SECOND THIRD
(Of both Old and New Yang Styles)

SLANT FLYING

We are told in the Classics of this posture that we must not forget that 'shoulder stroke' comes between these postures.

Blocking low against a right low attack you should grab the right wrist, step to behind his leading leg and throw him over your leading leg. Photo No. 118. You may also put a strike in with your shoulder before the throw. This is done on both sides.

No. 118   No. 119

FAIR LADY WORKS AT SHUTTLES

An attack is blocked with one arm, Photo No. 119. The other arm takes over and the first palm attacks to the chest as you step in. Photo No. 120.

SNAKE CREEPS DOWN

You should block and grab a left fist attack with your right palm, Photo No. 121. Then you should pull the opponent downward as you slip your left arm under the groin area

No. 120

No. 121

No. 122

No. 123

and attack the groin with shoulder. Photo No. 122. Another use for this posture is: You are being attacked with a right fist, you should block using p'eng with your right wrist and then your left palm grabs his right elbow. You then pull downward using your weight moving down. This is a most powerful technique and causes the opponent's head to hit the ground. Photo No. 123.

COCK STANDS ON ONE LEG

You should stand up quickly and grab a right or left fist attack with your appropriate palm as you use knee to the groin. Photo No. 124. From the 'Old Yang Style' we have two other uses for this posture. As the attack is imminent, you block it with your left palm and bring your other palm over the top to attack the face with palm slap and groin attack with your knee. Photo No. 125. Or, you could use your second palm to grab the throat after the block.

No. 124

No. 125

INSPECTION OF HORSES'S MOUTH

You block a left or right fist attack with your right palm and attack to the throat with finger jab. Photo No. 126.

ELBOW TWIST

This posture comes from the 'Old Yang Style'. Take an on-coming right punch and 'wrap it up' with both of your forearms. Use your elbow to break his elbow as you use your body as leverage. Photo No. 127.

No. 126

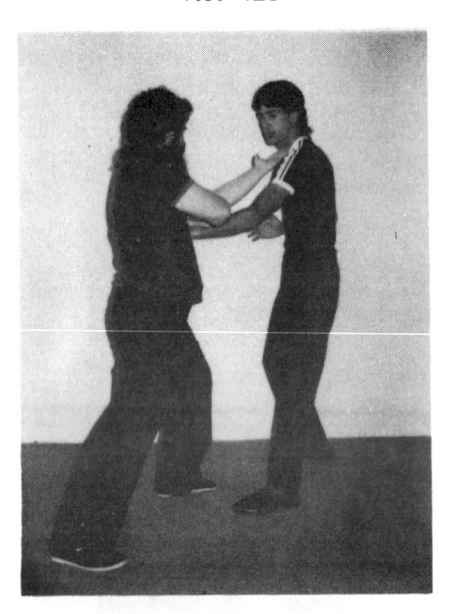

No. 127

HIDDEN HAND PUNCH

This also comes from the 'Old Yang Style'. Facing your opponent with your left foot forward he attacks with left punch low. You should leap into the air and block with your right forearm. Photo No. 128. You trap his arm with your left arm underneath your right arm and attack his lower abdomen with your left fist. Photo No. 129.

No. 128   No. 129

SLEEVES DANCING LIKE PLUMB BLOSSOMS
From the 'Old Yang Style': You are attacked with right fist, you should leap into the air and turn around while blocking with your left forearm. Photo No. 130. The other arm comes down like a windmill and attacks to the head. Photo No. 131.

STEP FORWARD TO SEVEN STARS
Step up and block as shown as you kick to the groin. Photo No. 132.

RIDING TIGER
Use this posture to evade and block a kick. Photo No. 133.

LOTUS KICK
Use your own two arms to attack the chest as your right leg comes across his lower back to 'break the roots'. Photo No. 134.

This concludes the uses of most of the postures from the New Yang Style of Yang Ching-Fu and the Old Yang Style as it was founded by Yang Lu-Chen (Lo-Sim).

The Old Yang Style is the style before it was changed to an all slow moving form in the mid 1920's. Yang Ching-Fu changed the form that was given to him by his Father some three times before he founded the now famous modern Yang Style, the most widely practised style in the world. For a complete history of t'ai chi (a realistic view), see my third book, "POWER T'AI CHI CH'UAN BOOK THREE".

As I stated in the introduction you must take the applications that I have given for their face value and take only what you need leaving the rest. As long as you know what the meaning is of each posture so that you are able to visualise when you perform the slow forms for their therapeutic value.

Some of these postures you will find will work in a real situation but I have found that it is much better to discover these for yourself. This is one of the pre-requisites in my school, we try to make leaders, not sheep.

No. 130   No. 131

PAGE SIXTY ONE

No. 132

No. 133

No. 134

END OF
CHAPTER
ONE

PUNCHING & KICKING

CHAPTER TWO

No matter what people think about kung-fu, in particular the internal styles, striking and kicking are still the main form of defence. We still 'yield' to an attack, we still use 'internal energy' rather than brute strength but in the end we use punching and kicking more than any other technique to finish a confrontation quickly and with the least amount of violence. Sometimes it is necessary to use some other technique such as grappling or locks and holds etc. but in the end the knock out punch or kick is the kindest way to stop a fight.

The main fights that any of us will encounter wil be the odd drunk at a party or the odd lout in the street, so we do not want to break his arm or leg to stop him from fighting, we try to stop him with the least amount of injury. If he gets up.... then we use something more.

It's all very well for me or anyone else to tell you that you must punch here or kick there but if you have never hit anyone then It usually comes as a big shock when you break your wrist on the first real punch or twist your ankle on the first real kick.

You need to punch quickly and with the most amount of power available. You need to be able to kick quickly and powerfully knowing that your first kick or punch will finish the confrontation. We have to know how to use the correct muscles for the right job and not have opposing muscles holding our fist or foot back.

T'AI CHI PUNCHING IS DIFFERENT

In T'ai Chi we try to use the least amount of energy to gain the greatest amount of work. To do this we have to know how to use the body and not just the arm to punch.

If we do not use any muscle power at all and just have a totally relaxed arm, we are able to turn the waist so that the arm will throw out at great speed like the principle of the whip. The handle and larger part of the rope is not travelling very fast but at the end when the whip cracks, that small end piece is like lightening and has much power. This is because there is a lot of energy being concentrated down into a small area. We use this same principle in punching. All we have to do is to control the fist using the least amount of muscle power so that it hits it's target.

In t'ai chi we use the last two knuckles, ie; the 'weakest' (or are they). Most so called 'hard styles' look in amazement when we use these knuckles to punch very hard objects with no damage to the bones. Wing-Chun uses these same bones but with the fist closed tightly so as not to damage the bones. After many years of practise we are able to use these knuckles without causing injury through lots of practise.

PRACTISE

You start out with a totally realaxed arm and palm, As you thrust forward with your rear foot, you twist your waist so that your shoulders turn quickly thrusting out your right or left palm . Just before impact you lightly close the fist and allow it to flick up at the end so that the last two knuckles are forced upward into the object being struck. You can gain this whipping action by pulling your fist backward quicker than it was thrown out. See Photo No. 135 for starting position and Photo No. 136 for end position. If you punch into a heavy bag, a good way to test if you are doing this punch correctly is to hit the bag into the general area that a face would be, (hard boney area) and if you cause a large poppin sound to happen upon impact without much, if any movement of the bag then you are doing it correctly. When punching to a face area and using the bag, there should not be much movement of the bag. We are looking for shock value and not pushing value. However, it is different when striking to the soft areas of the body. Now we must look for a movement of the bag when it is struck. We still do not allow too much follow through, we try to put a lot of energy into the bag to cause it to move

No. 135   No. 136

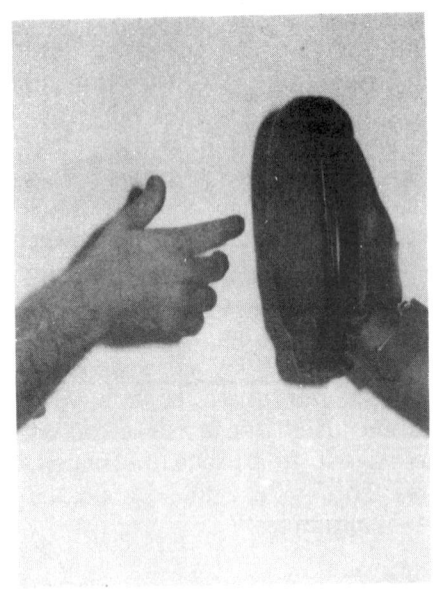

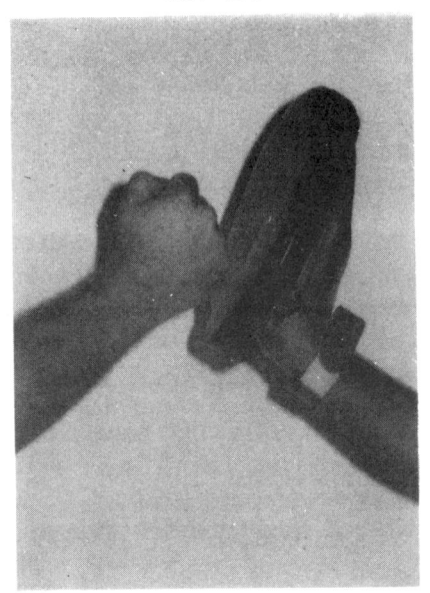

away with the least amount of forward movement from the punch. Photo No. 137.

One of the best training methods in boxing is the hard hand held mit. This is perfect for practising punching to the face. Now you must move the mit when you punch as far as possible with the least amount of arm movement. Try to strike the mit starting with your open fist only a few inches away. Don't try to push your fist out, try to move your body in a way that is enlikened to sneezing. This is what we call in t'ai chi a 'fajing' or explosive energy movement, the whole body must perform the action and not just one part.

Always remember to keep up your guard. When you punch with your right fist, keep your left palm over the right side of your face. When you punch with your left fist, keep your right palm over the left side of your face.

When you punch, push forward with the rear foot lifting the heel of that foot off the ground as seen in the last photo.

Punch the hand held mit five times with perfect timing and always bring the other palm back as a guard. Start out slowly

No. 137   No. 138

at first, trying to judge exactly how to place your fist so that you gain the maximum amount of power. Then, you start to speed up the five punches so that you are able to perform the five punches in about one second. However, you must keep the timing of the five punches exactly the same so that the time between each punch is the same. Also, and most importantly, you must be sure that you <u>aren't losing power in order to gain speed</u>, make sure that each punch is <u>felt</u> by the holder of the mit.

<u>USE YOUR WAIST AND NOT JUST YOUR ARMS</u>

Another excellent way of using equipment is to have someone hold two mits in front of you. You should strike the mit and then the other one. But, as soon as you have struck the first mit, your partner should move the second one to try and stop you from hitting it. This is excellent training for both striker and holder because the holder must be very aware of which mit is being struck first in order to move the other one. <u>Photo No. 138</u>.

DIFFERENT TYPES OF CENTRIFUGAL PUNCHING

All types of t'ai chi punches are called centrifugal because of the principle of the waist twisting to literally throw out the arm in a punch, this is centrifugal and allows one to use the strongest/fastest punch.

I have already covered the main 'straight' punch using the last two knuckles. This is one of the fastest punches and has much power over short distances and is good for in close fighting. You should be able to use this punch from most positions but if you are in a position where this punch is impossible there are some other punching techniques from t'ai chi.

THE STORK SPREADS WINGS PUNCH

This punch is one of the most powerful punches from any martial art. It is totally centrifugal and quite fast considering it's distance.

No. 139   No. 140

This is one of only three punches in t'ai chi that uses the first two knuckles. In t'ai chi we use the knuckles that most suit the position of the palm upon impact otherwise we use extra muscles to hold the palm into position and there-by lessen it's impact. The front jab as described earlier is not really a straight punch as aren't any of the t'ai chi punches. Upon impact the punch circles around and back so slightly that someone looking sees only a straight punch. This is why it is sometimes called a straight punch. The 'Stork Spreads Wings Punch' however looks circular from the beginning. As with most t'ai chi punches except the jab, it comes from a blocking movement. Although we usually defend and attack with all of our punches, this is the t'ai chi principle of defence rather than attack. Although, in effect, a bad word or a wrong look can be interpreted as an attack.

If you block with the right fist across to the left against a left face attack with the left palm underneath it, Photo No. 139, the left palm then takes over the block while the right fist is thrown out at the target with the turning of the waist. Photo No. 140. It's use is covered in chapter one.

No. 141   No. 142

CROSS PUNCH

This is one of the other punches that uses the first two knuckles. This punch is used to the hard boney areas and so it is a snapping punch. This also starts out from a block with the other hand, Photo No. 141. Notice the position of the punching hand before it punches. It is placed in a vertical position. When the body steps in and turns at the waist the palm is thrown out. Just before impact the waist is jerked back the other way which causes the fist to have the whip effect. You then flick the wrist over and form a light fist so that the wrist flicks into the object, Photo No. 142.

BACK FIST

This type of punch uses the back of the knuckles and is the easiest of all to understand the whipping principle. You should turn your waist (for a right handed punch) to the right and allow your fist to be thrown out. Just before impact, the waist is jerked back the other way so that the wrist is caused to whip out. You must have a totally relaxed wrist for this to work. You close your palm lightly upon impact. the forward motion doesn't have to be very fast, as it is the backward motion that is the main movement for this punch. Photo No. 143. Once again we always put in a block with this same fist before the attack. So if you're striking with the right fist, you would block across to your left with that same fist as if you are blocking a left handed punch.

BACK POWER PUNCH

This is a most powerful punch and is totally centrifugal. There is no pull back just before impact as it is aimed at the soft body areas. The whole arm must be totally relaxed as the body twists to give it centrifugal force. The arm swings out with the momentum of the body to strike with the back of the palm or you can form a light fist. Photo No. 144.

No. 143

No. 144

BACK SPINNING FIST

Unlike the back spinning kick which can become quite slow, the back spinning fist is very fast and quite powerful. It is the punch which uses the most centrifugal force. Once again for this to work with the greatest amount of power and speed the arm must be totally relaxed and you must take care not to strike the bag (or opponent) with your elbow, this will cause damage to your arm. You can either use an open palm or a fist. Step in with your left foot turned to your right and block an imaginary punch to your right. Photo No. 145. You step across in front of your opponent. Your right palm comes underneath your left one as you swivel on your both heels right around 180 degrees. This is your centrifugal force. Your right relaxed arm will spin out at great speed and power to strike the bag with great force. Photo No. 146. It will take some practise to get the swivel so that you are always in balance. You must totally relax with no power in your upper body, this will ground you so that you are centred. Your weight must change to your left foot upon impact.

PAGE SEVENTY

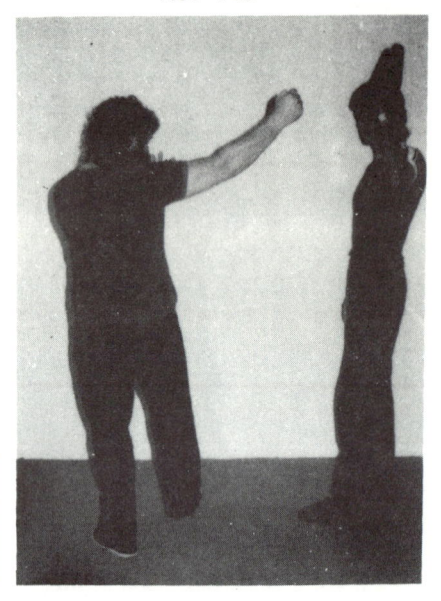

No. 145   No. 146

LOW REVERSE CIRCLE PUNCH

This punch is used to the lower abdomen and groin area and must be used with a blocking technique as it is not as fast as the others. With your right foot forward you block to your right with your left palm and as you do this you do a "change step' ie, your right foot is quickly withdrawn and your left foot is advanced. At the same time your right fist is drawn back in a circle and low. Photo No. 147. You now punch up into the lower part of the abdomen with the flat area of your fist. The palm side. Photo No. 148.

PENETRATION PUNCH

This is a very fast and powerful punch and is quite difficult to block as it is not quite straight or round. It is like a curved punch but on a much less arc.

Once again you block to the left, Photo No. 149. Then the right fist flicks out due to the turning of the waist and turns so that the small finger is upward upon impact. Photo No. 150.

No. 147 No. 148

No. 149 No. 150

In this section I have covered only a few of the easier punching technqiues from t'ai chi. There are others of course but they should be taught personally. I have covered more than enough punches to cover any situation. Practise on a bag by yourself at first to understand about timing and don't go too hard at first. Learn about relaxation and centrifugal force. Then ask someone to throw a few different attacks so that you are able to try them out in a more realistic situation. Keep in mind though, that nothing will prepare you for a real fight. So just because a few of your techniques start to work don't become over-confident.

POWER

Power is the most important aspect of any technique. If you are unable to knock an attacker down with your first punch then you will have to re-think your art. When you practise with a partner, try to punch right through his blocks so that you are able to lightly touch your target. This will also give your partner good practise at blocking more realistic attacks. This is most important as many martial artists only ever have practise in the school where-by the students don't throw full power punches. This is also where great control is necessary so that you do not knock your partner out. You must of course pull the attack short of the target so that no-one gets hurt. Or, you could invest in some GOOD protective equipment but even then control in necessary as nothing will stop percussion from a really strong attack.

KICKING

It is important for martial artists, especially of the 'internal schools' to be conversant with all of the regular kicking techniques in order to know how to defend against them. Too many t'ai chi practitioners use the cop-out of, "It isn't in the form so I don't have to learn it." The first thing that happens in a real situation is that his opponent uses a kick that he is not familiar with and so he is struck. I don't believe in using high flashy kicks but I do think that it's necessary to know how to use them. THe most devastating kicks are low to the legs, these are almost impossible to defend against especially if used in a defencive mode.

T'ai chi does have some of it's own kicking technqiues. These are usually kept low and simple and only used when we <u>know</u> that they will work. Usually we will use the excellent hand techniques for some time, this puts our opponent at ease in thinking that we do not use kicks, then we will put in a stomack heel kick or one to the chest and it usually works.

SOME KICKS

THE FRONT HEEL KICK

This kick is the simplest kick of all but it is also one of the most difficult to execute correctly. Usually upon trying this kick for the first time, your foot will glance upward on the bag with not much effect until you discover that you must thrust the waist inward so that your heel is snapped in towards the target and not up and away from it. <u>Photo No. 151.</u> Always put in the particular palm movement with this kick as you should always block before attacking.

THE SIDE SNAP OR CRESCENT KICK

This is the first kick in the Yang ChingFu all slow moving form and uses either the instep or the knife-edge of the foot. You must twist your waist so that your leg below the knee is thrown out at great speed and snaps in onto the target, either low at the knee or higher to the kidney area. You can go higher to the face but this is not advised. <u>Photo No. 152.</u>

THE LEG SNAP KICK

This is the kick that is meant when we use the 'heel stance' in the t'ai chi form. It is very powerful, fast and probably the best one that you will ever use. It is almost impossible to block. The waist plays a very important part in giving the leg the centrifugal force. <u>Photo No. 153.</u>

PAGE SEVENTY FOUR

No. 151

No. 152

No. 153

No. 154

GROIN KICK

This kick is represented by the 'toe stances' from the form and is used to the groin using the instep. Groin kicks can be either devastating or not work at all. Only try this kick if you are really sure that you will hit the target. Photo No. 154.

BACK KICK

This kick comes from 'The Old Yang Style' and I find it one of the best defencive kicks apart from the leg kicks. It is usually aimed at the lung area or just under the arm. This is a good kick to use all by itself to defend against a punch to the head. Photo No. 155.

BACK TURNING HEEL KICK

This kick comes from the t'ai chi short stick form and is an excellent defencive kick. It can also be used in conjunction with a feint. It is fast, powerful and done correctly is un-telegraphic.

Firstly, step in with your left foot (or right as the case may be), and block with your left palm turning your left foot inward as shown in Photo No. 156. Now turn your waist around and thrust the right foot inward to the stomach area. Photo No. 157.

BACK SPINNING HEEL KICK

This kick can work in a defencive mode but forget it in an attacking mode unless your opponent knows nothing about the martial arts. It works the same as for the 'Back Turning heel kick' but instead of the right foot being thrust inward in a back kick, the foot is swung out using the waist for centrifugal force. The contact is made by the back of the heel as it swings into the target. It is fairly easy to block if you are aware and move in very quickly at the instant that it is instigated. Photo No. 158.

ROUNDHOUSE KICK

This is the kick that is most used by kickboxers in tournaments so it should not be used in the street unless you are really sure that you aren't going to receive a broken or

PAGE SEVENTY SIX

No. 155

No. 156

No. 157

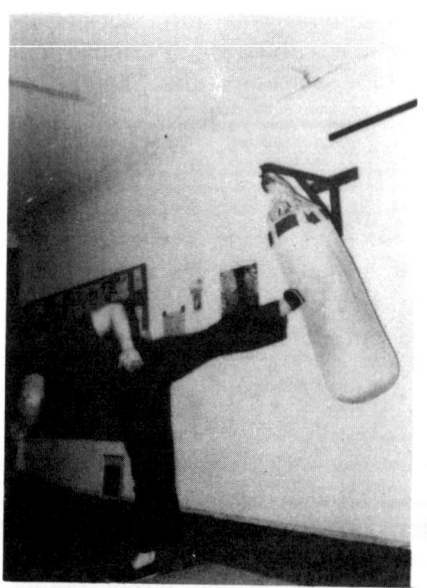

No. 158

badly bruised shin from a well timed elbow. This is one good way to block this type of kick.

Your front leg is lifted as shown in Photo No. 159. You now twist your rear heel inward and roll your hip over to flick the right foot out in a snapping motion from the knee. Photo No. 160. You must also try a double kick so that you will know how to block it. Use a roundhouse kick to the leg using no heel twist but gain the power from the waist, then bounce the same leg upward to attack to the upper body or face using the heel twist.

No. 159   No. 160

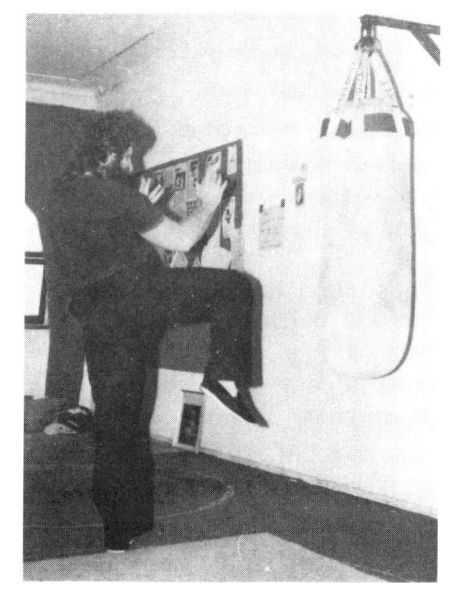

TRAINING METHODS

It'a all very well to practise these techniques in the classroom but when it comes to using them you will have to know exactly what it will feel like for real. The most important thing in kicking is to know that a kick will work.

Firstly we work with a partner. We use slow, well aimed heel kicks to the knee area, not right on the top of the knee but to the side to break the ligaments that hold the lower leg on. Have your partner come at you as if to attack slowly, then step to where-ever you feel is the right place to gain the correct timing and kick to his knee. Make sure that your heel is used each time and that you have hit the exact spot each time. Photo No. 161. After some time when you are sure that every kick is making it's mark, start to get a little faster but be careful not to hurt each other. The attacker will tell you if the kicks are striking at the correct point. After some time you will be able to use a medium bag to protect your leg as your partner kicks at full force onto the bag. Remember! POINT YOUR KNEE INTO THE FORCE SO THAT NO DAMAGE OCCURS. This is the closest thing to a real kick that you can aim for without really kicking someone. Photo No. 162.

The same thing can be done for kicks to the body. Hold the bag over the appropriate area and allow your partner to kick the bag using all of the above technqiues except the back spinning heel kick. Train this one on the hanging bag.

Another useful leg kick is a sort of back kick to the leg. As your partner comes in, you should step out and use back kick onto his knee. Photo No. 163.

Everyone has a favourite leg kick so find the one most suited to you and use it. Then keep using it until it is perfect and has become sub-conscious. You should use only a few techniques and leave the rest for fun. In a real situation you have to be very sure that your two or three technqiues will work. Leave out all of the fancy leg sweeps etc, they might work in the classroom but in the street it's a different story. Kick to the legs and you will be alright.

BLOCKING KICKS

As stated earlier, leg kicks are the hardest of all to block and so I will start with blocking these kicks.

I will be covering 'sticking hands' (the t'ai chi version) later. I mention this because this is also where we learn to block low knee kicks, or at least try.

Two people stand as shown in Photo No. 164. Keeping your wrists lightly touching, you now start to move around. One

PAGE SEVENTY NINE

No. 161

No. 162

No. 163

No. 164

player should kick slowly to the knee of the other. You should be aware of the kick and pull your leg back quickly. Photo No. 165. I learnt this technique from an old arnis master in Manila, the difference was that they would strike at each other's legs with the sticks. You must not look at your opponent's feet, always take in the whole body using your periferal vision as later you will also be putting in hand techniques. After only a short period of this type of practise you will be able to perceive the attacks quicker and so you will be able to speed up the attacks. After you have evaded the attack you will be able to re-attack to his knee with another kick. The most important thing in this training is not to allow it to become a melé, keep it cool and learn.

BLOCKING KICKS ABOVE THE KNEES

All other kicks can be blocked with the palms and elbows. The elbow is a formidable weapon against kicks and stops anyone from using flashy roundhouse kicks. For all other kicks we use 'the barging technqiue.' This is a most excellent training method that will work in a real situation.

If someone is going to kick you, he will have to have his timing/distance right in order to deliver the right amount of power at the right time. If you are adept at very quickly moving in at the exact moment, the kick will become inefectual. You might be struck but the force will be halved.

ATTACK THE ATTACKING PORTION

This is a good training method against kicks and has also to do with the barging technique. You are inevitably going to be kicked in the stomach so we train to be kicked in the stomach. As your partner kicks you, (gently) into your stomach you should have the idea that you will attack his foot with your stomach. When you are struck, 30% of the effect of the strike is the shock value. As you are about to be struck move in onto the kick and breathe out and as you do this use reverse breath. ie; you breathe out and the lower abdomen is pushed out, not inward as is the normal way of breathing. You attack his foot and push him away. After some time the kicks can become a little harder until you are able to pretty well defend against a medium power kick. It is of course much better to have used the barging technique in conjunction with a block so that you aren't struck at all but this technqiue trains you for when you are struck and enables you to keep going.

The barging technqiue is just what it's name implies, we barge in and attack the opponent as he kicks us using a block to move the attacking leg away and so put him off balance. His timing is put off and so is the kick, even if it does strike, it only has about 50% power. We are then able to take the offencive and attack with a sub-conscious reaction.

For front kicks we have someone kick us and usually block in a circle with one palm. Photo No. 166. This is also a pa-kua technqiue. We are now able to re-attack either that same leg to the knee, Photo No. 167, or to the face or body, Photo No. 168.

For the roundhouse kick we block upward with both palms, Photo No. 169. Notice the position of your own elbow, it is used to damage the shin of the on-coming leg. Then we barge in with both arms pounding down onto his body. Photo No. 170.

You should experiment with these techniques to find out which one suits you the best. The whole idea of blocking is based solely upon your being aware and this only comes with countless hours of controlled practise. The moment your attacker has even thought of the attack you barge in and re-attack, this is how we train to defend against kicks. The arms do nothing special they just throw out in a circular block, then because we used a circular block we are able to bring it back to attack. This is what is meant by balanced Yin and Yang techniques.

You must remember that no technique is perfect and some time in your martial arts training you will be hit, this is the best experience that you can have, you are then at least ready for it when it happens again, and it will. For this purpose we use boxing gloves and protective equipment in sparring.

In order to stop our training from becoming a melé we have one person attacking trying to strike the other, while the other will only block and try to get in as close to his attacker as possible to win. The attacker will try and strike the attackee to stop him from coming in. Later and only when both players are ready, we go on to full sparring under supervision. As soon as one player makes a mistake the instructor should stop the match and everyone should talk about that mistake. Do

PAGE EIGHTY TWO

No. 165

No. 166

No. 167

No. 168

No. 169   No. 170

not go on to full sparring too soon as this will only keep you back at a low level. Only when you are ready must you even think about sparring. Even then you must train in sparring for only a short time then get back to basics again. The more you practise the basics, the greater your advanced skills will increase.

Any instructor worth his salt will get in there and box with the students, in this way he is able to completely control that particular student's evolution into a good boxer. Only occasionally should student be put in against student, and then it must be under strict supervision. The match should be stopped when the instructor notices that either player is becoming aggressive or competitive. We learn a martial art so that we are able to defend ourselves and our families not to compete against each other or to build up egos.

SPARRING

CHAPTER THREE

The best exercise that two people can practise for awareness and to understand sparring is push hands. I have covered the main areas of this exercise in my second book, "POWER T'AI CHI CH'UAN BOOK TWO" so I will not cover it here. I will say though that push hands should be learnt for the sake of learning a martial art and not for the sake of doing push hands. The real way of push hands is quite different to what many people think it is. The whole idea of push hands has to do with balance, weighting and power. One shouldn't have the idea of 'I can push you but you can't push me.' So what! we learn push hands to know about a 'method of fighting'.

I will cover in this book an advanced method and probably the best method of leading a student into sparring called 'T'ai Chi Sticking Hands.' Along with the pakua method of sticking hands we have an unsurpassed way of learning about sparring.

Sticking hands teaches us about close in fighting and that's where it really counts, we don't fight someone from 10 feet away. You are being attacked from only inches away and you must block the attack and immediately re-attack until it becomes as close to reflex action as possible. Once again the main thing is not to allow this to become a brawl, this way no-one learns. We must use great control and try to become super sensitive. Even if it means that we are defeated many times to gain this sensitivity it will be worth it in the end. I will add here that this type of sticking hands has nothing to do with the Wing-Chun version.

Your arms must be totally relaxed, using only the right amount of muscle to hold them up there. If you are attacked you must immediately change to yin, ie; you relax your attacking portion and re-attack using the folding principle. I will cover this very important t'ai chi aspect later. I was invited to attend a workshop given by Dan Innosanto so that I was able to write an article for the Magazine, "Australasian Fighting Arts" for which I have my own column, and I found that Dan was using more t'ai chi principles in his training than many t'ai chi practitioners, in particular the folding principle.

If you ever have the chance to study with Dan Innosanto take it as I regard him as one of the foremost martial artists of our time.

STICKING HANDS

Two people face each other as for push hands but with wrists touching. Photo No. 171. You should start to rotate your palms as if churning butter on a flat plane. The person who's hands are on the top should attack to the face of the other who should block this attack outward to either side of his head. Photo No. 172. The person who's hands are underneath should attack to the other's lower abdomen who blocks it downward and out to either side. Photo No. 173. At no time should the wrists break contact. When this has been practised for some time

No. 171   No. 172

No. 173　　　　　　　　No. 174

you are then able to change the position of your palms at will but still keeping contact. So, you might have your right palm on the top and you wish to move it under. You would use an attack to the lower abdomen as you do this. Photo No. 174. At the same time your partner can block this attack and immediately re-attack to your face or abdomen. This is the crux of this exercise, you MUST always re-attack as close to simultaneously as possible with the attacker's movement. If you block with the right hand outward, then slam it back down onto his head or, if your other palm is closer, use that one. You must take the shortest route to re-attack. If your partner is able to get in a good solid attack then you do not follow up as he has defeated you but if you have blocked his attack then you must re-attack. Then he must block that attack and also re-attack. This continues until a solid blow has landed. When I say a solid blow I mean one that if it were for real would knock your opponent out and not just a light slap to the face etc.

Your palms must keep circling around your opponent's until you are able to 'gain the upper hand.' You may use arm grabs, locks, throws, kicks as already covered in the section on kicking. You may grab both of his palms and bring his chest down onto your knee. In this case if you are the attackee, you must go with the force and never against it. So, you would come in towards your opponent barge in as you block the knee and attack with shoulder. In this way you use the opponent's force against him. You can use pushes, in fact anything just as long as you never lose contact. Keep your arms relaxed. Keep your teeth closed! This is good sense in any situation whether it is sparring in the school or in a real situation. Keep cool and most importantly don't become angry. YOU ARE THERE TO HELP EACH OTHER, NOT TO COMPETE!

After some time you will be able to start moving around while still keeping contact at the wrists. Now it becomes really tricky, you must be aware of kicks to the legs, head and body attacks as well as throws, locks and holds and higher kicks. And this is happening as you are busy looking after your own balance while moving. This is one of the greatest kung-fu training methods for all martial artists.

THE FOLDING PRINCIPLE

This principle is solely based upon your changing from yin to yang. If you walk to the top of a hill, then you have gone as far yang as possible. If you stay there you will be unable to go anywhere unless you come down again. In other words you must go yin before you are able to do any more work. It's the same with punching and indeed the whole of your t'ai chi training. We must be forever changing in order to re-attack after being blocked. If I punch someone and that punch is successfully blocked as in Photo No. 175, and if I leave my arm in a yang state ie; in the attacking state, the arm is useless unless I do something to change it's state to yin. This is where the folding principle comes in . When my punch is blocked I should totally relax it and allow it to 'fold up' with the nat-momentum of his block as in Photo No. 176. Now I am able to bring this same fist back into a yang mode and re-attack as in Photo No. 177. Notice that I have also blocked the arm that has blocked me downward with my other palm. This sort of technique takes only a split second and is an excellent training device.

PAGE EIGHTY EIGHT

No. 175

No. 176

No. 177

No. 178

THE METHOD

Two people stand opposite each other and one throws a punch as already shown, the punch is blocked as shown. The attacker should allow his arm to automatically fold up and become yin. In order not to get into the habit of pulling your fist back using your own muscles, the blocker should not always block the punch, making sure that the attacker does not pull his arm back on purpose. It must be the momentum of the block that causes the arm to fold up. You can do this with the attacker blindfolded, this way he doesn't know when you are going to block and has to rely upon his own feeling.

Next, you should try to block the attackee's blocking arm downward with your left palm and re-attack with your right fist as seen in photo No. 177. The right palm should come up underneath the left one which blocks downward from the top. This is the principle of continuous punching. What ever portion of the attacker's body is used to block your attack you re-block it and re-attack usually with the same fist until you have broken through all of your opponent's first and second line of defence and are able to attack his third line, the body. You can play around with this forever and always learn from it. Just keep on blocking the hand that has blocked you and re-attack. You must remain relaxed so that your attacks can become simultaneous and sub-conscious after much practise. The classics say of the folding principle; "If the elbow is caught, circle it back and strike with the back of the fist for equal success." OR, "The method for breaking locks lies in the wrist." This tells us that the folding principle also works with locks. If we are grabbed on the wrist and pulled downward, we shouldn't try to use force to pull our palm free, we should relax the wrist and turn it in the direction of the least resistance, usually against the thumb. Then we should re-attack usually with elbow or shoulder. During push hands if your wrist is grabbed, simply turn it over relaxed. Your timing must be perfect otherwise you will be caught. If you stay yang, this gives the opponent something to hold onto on order to control your body. Try for yourself. Hold your arm tense and ask someone to pull or push your palm. Your whole body will be controlled through your arm. But if you relax your arm, your opponent has nothing with which to control you and in this short time you have already re-attacked. You don't of course leave your arm yin so that he can re-attack it, staying yin is just as dangerous as staying yang, you must change from yin to yang in order to re-attack. If your wrist is caught (because your timing was off) you should relax it (fold it) and come in using either elbow or shoulder stroke to his mid-section or chest. People just don't expect us to 'go with the force' so they are usually taken by surprise when you barge inward with shoulder.

DA-LU

This principle of da-lu can also be used in a fighting way It says in the classics of da-lu or the 'four corners';
"With erroneous technique one has no choice but to use the four corners to help return to the framework of squareness and roundness."
This means that 'pull down, split, elbow stroke and shoulder stroke' make up for deficiencies in our technique. If we happen to be pulled off balance because we are deficient, we must go with the force using a step to the corner then re-direct the movement to bring us back into the opponent and use either elbow or shoulder. So if I am attacked as shown in Photo No. 178, I should take a step with my left foot to the side in the direction of the momentum and push back at an angle using elbow or shoulder. The classics say that this is only used if my cardinal line of defence, (the folding technique) is not yet perfect. So t'ai chi gives some techniques to save ourselves until we have learnt the right way of using the principles.

BEGINNING SPARRING

It is not an easy matter to begin to fight. Human beings on the whole would really prefer not to fight but sometimes we have to through no fault of our own. This is why we use the excellent training method of t'ai chi and pa-kua sticking hands. These methods allow us to 'get the feel of fighting' without feeling as if we're threatened in any way or in some sort of competition. It allows one to relax and find the correct way rather than just fighting and therefore staying at one level. Slowly these training techniques become more and more like free sparring until eventually you break the contact and you are free sparring before you know it. It is very important not to go into sparring too soon. If you try sparring and you just tense up and have a feeling of competition then stop and go back to basics, you're not ready for it. However, if you try it and you really feel at home and not under any threat, then you are ready for free sparring. In the beginning just keep it very easy and don't try too much to knock your partner's head off, just use each other to learn. Start with semi-contact, ie; you are able to strike certain areas with a reasonable force without really doing any damage. As you become more at ease, put on the gloves and try some more substansial power. The most important thing even in non-contact is not to use less power in order not to hit someone. You must use as much power as possible so that your partner is able to know what a powerful attack is like. So many martial arts schools fiddle around with a flick here and a flick there and when someone puts in a full powered attack they don't know what hit them.

PA-KUA SPARRING

I am including this technique from pa-kua because it is without doubt one of the best ways of learning about fighting without really hurting anyone. The wrists are in contact and it is controlled in the beginning with each player just learning about him/herself and their technique.

Two players stand opposite each other and join palms at the wrists over the centre of a circle. Photo No. 179. Without going into the rather peculiar pa-kua walking style as it is not really necessary when only taking this exercise for it's learning sparring value, you start to walk in a circle keeping your wrists over the centre of the circle. You must only have a light touch. If you are walking in a clockwise direction with your right wrists touching, you now perform the 'inside turn.' This means that with your left foot in the forward position you swivel both toes back towards the right rear so that you are now facing the other direction. You must also change the position of your palms in order to now have your left wrists touching. Your right palm is seen as the block and as you turn, your left palm is seen as an attack to his face. Photo No. 180. Who-ever initiates the movement is the attacker and the other is the

No. 179   No. 180

blocker. The other player's left palm was used to block your left palm.

The outside turn is next to learn. If you are travelling in a clockwise direction and wish to turn to walk the other way but your right foot is forward, you cannot perform the inside turn. You must now swivel almost 360° on the heels to face the opposite direction. Your left palm now uses the centrifugal force when the body swings around. This too is an attack to the face or body and a block depending on who initiates the attack. Photo No. 181.

You would never in a real situation turn your back on the opponent without reason to do so. In order to keep this rule we do something to the opponent's arm before turning around.

From the previous clockwise position before attacking with the outside turn you should flick his palm with great force to your left as you attack. Photo No. 182. From this position you are able to use any number of attacking and defence techniques. We are able to use any type of kick, Photo No. 183. You are able to use punches, locks and holds or throws as in Photo No. 184.

PAGE NINETY THREE

No. 181

No. 182

No. 183

No. 184

I have only covered this pa-kua technique briefly as it is an excellent introduction to sparring. Once you have been practising this technique for some time, you may break the wrists apart and do it in a more realistic way. The circling teaches us to come in at an angle rather than meet force on force.

It takes a long time to use the internal arts in a fighting way and the training to get there is hard. But if you stick it out, you will gain great benefits, the least of which is great good health and great fighting ability.

END OF CHAPTER THREE

To be elated at success and disappointed at failure is to be the child of circumstances: how can such a one be called the master of anything if he is not the master of himself.

Never call any man or woman your master, they might be a master but no-one is your master.
Be your own master

THE CLASSICS

CHAPTER FOUR

Most classical Chinese martial arts are able to be traced back to their various beginnings by some tangible means such as ancient drawings and script. This is most true of the Shaolin derived martial arts. On the other hand we have the internal Chinese martial arts where we find that not much in the way of tangible evidence, drawings etc, has been left to us. All that we have to follow for the most part is the lineage principle where-by the Father taught the son or each master only took on one or two trusted disciples. Some of these disciples did however write down all of their thoughts on the internal arts as they learnt them and so nowadays we are left with many classical sayings and poems which have been translated many times from ancient Chinese to middle Chinese to modern Chinese then into English and many Eupopean languages.

The principle of the Classic is most evident in the internal martial art of t'ai chi ch'uan where we are left with many classic sayings and poems written by various masters since the beginning of the art. Even today, all we are able to test our knowledge with are these classics and many arguments have resulted in different translations as to how certain postures or techniques should be performed etc.

There are two ways that we are able to look at the classics. Firstly we are able to take them as they are in their literal sense, or we are able to take them as back up to our own evolution. I prefer to use the later method and use the classics as back up to my own evolution of t'ai chi. Of course in the beginning we must follow the teachings of a competant master in order to learn the basic movements and some of his/her ideas etc, but if we stay as disciples, we stay as sheep and never evolve our own ideas and take the art right back to it's beginning and learn for ourselves what the old masters learnt for themselves. If we are to take any internal martial art which is largely based upon unseen internal forces back to it's beginning then we must have some idea of what the old masters were thinking. For this purpose we have their own thoughts, the classics.

There have been many translations of the classics but the ones that give the most correct versions are those that use as little English language licence as possible and only use direct translations. In this way we are able to allow the words to enter our minds and give us a helping hand only when we are ready to receive the correct information. This is because this person is at a basic level of understanding, however, if this same person reads that same classsic writing at a much later time in his/her development then they may receive what the classics have to offer. If your martial art is to be truly your own then you must take it right back to it's beginning and learn what the masters learnt.

THE CLASSICS ARE OUR WAY BACK:

Many arguments have arisen as to exactly what the initial use was for t'ai chi ch'uan, whether for martial or for healing etc. Or many arguments still exist today as to what the use is for certain postures or how to turn the foot etc. All one has to do is to read the classics to find the answers. If you do not find the answers then you just aren't ready to be given the answers.

T'ai Chi Classics

The t'ai chi classics were written by many masters of years gone by, some were well known, some were unknown, some were anonymous.

As to the use of t'ai chi we hear from one of the most famous Yang Style masters, Yang Pan-Hou who's Father invented the Yang Style.

"Hit the opponent's chest with single whip." or for the posture of 'Stork Spreads Wings,' "Parry and hit the opponent's soft areas and use no mercy." or, "Step up parry and punch to the ribs and protect your centre with 'close up.'"

Quite obviously when this classic was written, the master had the martial application in mind. By the time that Yang Ching-Fu wrote his classics, we start to see a softening of the classics. Yang Ching-Fu was the nephew of Yang Pan-Hou. By the time that later masters after Yang Ching-Fu wrote their classics we see a leaning towards the great healing benefits of t'ai chi. The later master did write about the martial aspects as well and most still regard t'ai chi as a martial art which has great health benefits.

Many of the classics are written in poetic form and can only be understood if the reader is up to a certain mind level.

"Execute play the pipa and use threading and transforming energy." Or, "In moving to and fro, us the folding method in advancing and retreating use changes and turning."

Many classics are quite clear in what they are trying to transmit. "The method of cross legs, breaks the softer bone below the knee." Some classics have slightly esoteric meanings such as, "If there is hardness within our softness we will never be defeated, if our hardness contains no softness, it can never be called firm."

Some of the classics give us exact details as to the postures of t'ai chi. "Before slant flying, use shoulder stroke." This tells us that shoulder should be used before and in between each slant flying posture something that many Yang styles have left out.

The classics give us explainations on how to use every facet of t'ai chi from the form through to push hands and street fighting. If we are able to understand them and use them as back-up to our own learning then they are the greatest learning tool available to any t'ai chi student. If we take them all as literal and never question or experiment, not keeping what we want and losing the rest then we will become as sheep and never become our own masters.

A most excellent translation of the classics is by Douglas Wile in his book, "T'ai Chi Touchstones." This book is a must for all who practise the martial art of t'ai chi ch'uan.

LONG HAR CH'UAN

CHAPTER FIVE

I said earlier that 'Long Har Ch'uan' is where we learn to forget about technique and take all that we have learnt and put it inside. This is where our technique becomes sub-conscious so that our body and mind can work as one unit. This method must not be taken for actual fighting technique because then it becomes just that, another technique to learn. We must treat this as a training device to teach us something. Some of these techniques could very well be used as fighting techniques but we prefer them to become sub-conscious reactions rather than a planned line of defence.

This is the hardest of all areas for people to learn, especially those who have studied another 'external' martial art. The most common questions asked by students from other schools is 'What If!' We call these the what if brigade. I always invite new students to DO WHAT IF and see what happens, then they say "But you did something completely different!" Then I explain that the techniques that they are learning must not be taken as strict rule, they are only training devices. Devices that teach us to change our line of defence automatically as the fighting situation changes. 'No Form' means that we change to suit the form of the attacker, this is what is meant by 'sticking to and not letting go' from the classics.

THE METHOD

The first technique from long har ch'uan is the folding principle which I have already covered.

THE VERTICAL METHOD

Sometimes we call this method 'Australian Boxing' because it resembles the swatting of flies from one's face. Two players stand opposite each other in an easy for them stance or rather 'no stance.' The attacker throws a face punch with his right fist as the attackee blocks it with a sort of stroking motion across his body with his right palm to cause the fist to just miss his face. Photo No. 185. If we were to use a pushing type of block and push the fist some distance to the left, this would give the attacker some considerable reaction time in which to counter. Notice that the body has turned slightly to your left as the left palm immediately and almost simultaneously comes up underneath the right palm to take over the block. Photo No. 186.

No. 185   No. 186

The right palm then continues down to your right side to block his second attack low to your right rib area. Photo No. 187. This all happens in an instant with the second attack coming in as fast as it is possible for the attacker to bring it in after his first attack. Then to finish off, you should turn your waist to your right and attack his face with left fist. In practise we use the chest as this exercise becomes very fast. Photo No. 188. You should hear four distinct sounds as you perform the four movements. The last two techniques, the low block and the fist attack should not be simultaneous but a split second between them. The whole technique should only take a fraction of a second to execute once you have mastered

No. 187   No. 188

the movements. Do it as many times as you like in order to learn it correctly. Then do the whole practise on the other side.

Once you have mastered both sides you do five on the right and five on the left not stopping to change direction. This of course leads to your attacker being able to attack at any time on any side with you blocking on either side. Once you have mastered this then you start to move around as if your attacker is really trying to attack you from any side with you blocking on any side, still using the two punches. This goes on to more advanced techniques but it can be seen that this amount will keep you busy for quite some time and is an excellent training method for awareness, sensitivity and fighting ability.

The next facet of the vertical plane is to have your partner throw two face punches one after the other. This time instead of blocking downward with your right (or left) palm, you should block upward and then punch. Photo No. 189. There is no difference from the first way except that you block upward on the second attack. Now you are able to combine left and right attacks with upper or lower second attacks so it becomes quite

No. 189   No. 190

a handful for both players.

THE LATERAL METHOD

The next area of 'long har ch'uan is the lateral block and defends against two head punches, one after the other.

THE METHOD

Two players face each other as before. One player throws a left head punch. The other should quickly block with his right palm and bring his left palm under it ready as shown in Photo No. 190. The body turns to the left as your left palm takes over the block to your left. Photo No. 191. Now he throws another face punch with his right fist. Your right palm is ready in position so you twist your waist to your right taking his punch over to the right as you strike to his face with your left palm. Photo No. 192. Once again this all happens in a split second with the attacker throwing the punches as quickly as possible. You are now able to change sides at will for instance, you could block with your left palm after the first attack and then take over the block with your right palm, then as

No. 191   No. 192

the right fist comes in, you should take it with your left palm, and strike with your right palm.

After some time this sort of block and re-attack will become totally natural because it is! Then you are able to use any of the above techniques very quickly while moving. You will also find that you are able to use any part of any one of the techniques at any time to defend against any attack.

MULTIPLE ATTACKS

This is also a part of 'long har ch'uan' and teaches us to attack many times not only once, the idea being that if you are able to strike once, then why not a number of times.

THE METHOD
           One player attacks with a straight punch to the face. The other player firstly blocks on the 'closed side' using his left palm. Photo No. 193. Then his left palm sort of strokes the arm downward as his right palm takes over while the left palm strikes to the face. Photo No. 194. Then the left palm takes over as the right palm strikes to the face, Photo No. 195.

No. 193   No. 194

And this goes on with each palm stroking the arm downward while the other one strikes. This is very fast and only needs practise for it to become very fast and useful.

You should always try to block onto the open side of your attacker. However, sometimes this is impossible and so we must know what to do when we must block onto his open or dangerous side. The other palm must be blocked as well even if it isn't attacking. As in the vertical blocking techniques already covered.

If the opponent is quite tall you would not attack his face because this will bring you in very close to him, having to reach upward to reach his face. In this case you would probably strike at the acupuncture points under the arm. Photo No. 196.

In this last section I have touched briefly on 'Long Har Ch'uan.' This is enough to get you started. Much of this advanced fighting art of t'ai chi can only be taught personally. If you find that for some reason it doesn't work, then you are doing something wrong because these techniques are known to work from my own experience.

No. 195   No. 196

END OF CHAPTER FIVE

HOW DO YOU FEEL NOW THAT YOU HAVE BEEN PROCLAIMED TO BE ENLIGHTENED. one monk asked of the other.   JUST AS ROTTEN AS EVER. he replied.

SOME OTHER TECHNIQUES

CHAPTER SIX

In this chapter I will be covering some other techniques that have a proven track record. These techniques are taught in my advanced boxing class.

We have called our boxing class 'no frills boxing' because if something does not work then we throw it out. Only very basic, one technique movements are kept, then we are sure that when we need it, our 'no technique method' will not let us down.

WRIST GRABBING

I have already covered how to break from a wrist grab. Now I will show you some training methods that allow you to grab a wrist after someone has attacked with a punch. This is one of the hardest things to do, especially if the person attacking knows the 'folding principle.' Many schools that rely upon wrist locks and grabs just don't practise these techniques in a realistic way, try putting in a really fast snap punch and see if anyone is able to catch it. We do have a training method that will at least give you a chance. If you are able to learn the wrist grab, a whole new area of defence will arise.

THE METHOD

You will again need a partner. Have your partner throw a medium pace punch with his right arm. You should block upward using p'eng, Photo No. 197. You now very quickly try to use your right palm to grab his wrist. This is tricky and requires some amount of practise. Your right palm must clamp down onto his wrist with a slipping motion, don't try to grab his wrist outright, allow your right palm to slip slightly down his forearm as it tightens the grip. This of course takes a fraction of a second. If you find that you are able to do this easily at that pace, your partner must increase his speed until you can no longer grab his arm, now stay at that speed until you are able to catch it.

PAGE ONE HUNDRED AND SIX

No. 197

No. 198

No. 199

No. 200

SOME P'ENG TECHNIQUES

From the above p'eng block you are able to try many techniques. The first is a simple but effective technique called 'choy.' Choy means 'inch energy' and uses the power of the waist to jerk the wrist after the grab in order to put the neck out or dislocate the shoulder. Photo No. 198. A further advancement of choy is to use the knee as shown. Photo No. 199. This can expand for a bit of over-kill to use the palm to the face. Photo No. 200. The use of the elbow is also quite effective and an extremely good weapon to train. It can also be used after p'eng as in Photo No. 201. The arm lock can be used after p'eng as shown in Photo No. 202. This can be advanced into figure four hammer lock as in Photo No. 203.

A useful take down technique from p'eng makes use of the opening posture of the form.

THE METHOD

Block using p'eng and quickly move in behind your opponent to take him down as shown. Photo No. 204.

Many good techniques can happen from p'eng, it is a very useful technique to know. But it requires much practise.

No. 201					No. 202

PAGE ONE HUNDRED AND EIGHT

No. 203

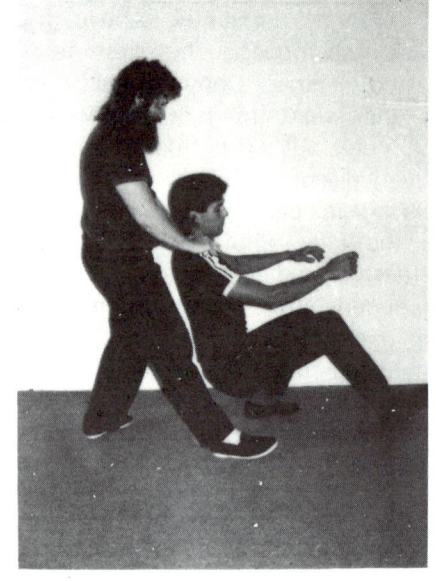

No. 204

No. 205

No. 206

No. 207   No. 208

TECHNIQUES FROM LONG HAR CH'UAN

Although long har ch'uan is essentially a training method, it does have some useful techniques that work.

From the closed side the opponent attacks with right fist. You should step to your left side and block as shown in Photo No. 205. Your right palm takes over the block from underneath while your left fist strikes at his axila area. Photo No. 206. From the same attack you can also use the right elbow to the same area. Photo No. 207.

An interesting take down comes from long har ch'uan. As you are attacked by his right fist you should use the first part of the vertical long har ch'uan technique Photo No. 208. Then you should turn your left palm to grab his right wrist as your forearm is jammed into his elbow. Photo No. 209. Now using the momentum of your body, you use his elbow as leverage to take him down. Photo No. 210. When done correctly the opponent's feet will come right off the ground. This technique can also be done on the 'closed' side for greater effect. You should use the same initial block only on the closed side,

No. 209   No. 210

ie; onto his left arm. Then use the same technique to break his elbow. Photo No. 211.

Another use for the posture 'lift hands' is to take a right fist with your left palm on the outside and slam your right thumb into the soft area of his bi-cep. The thumb should be bent on top of your fist as normal. Photo No. 212.

A curved or roundhouse punch is the most common punch used by an 'untrained' fighter and this technique will be useful against these attacks. As he comes in for the attack open both of your arms, one to block his attack, the other to strike across his chest or neck. Photo No. 213. Now with your arm pressed across his neck you are able to take him down. Photo No. 214.

Another nice take down from p'eng involves taking a block using p'eng and using the other palm to grab his wrist. You should use the momentum of your body to make an arc downward as you throw his wrist along that arc. His body will follow. Photo No. 215.

BEND BACKWARDS

This technique is used by many martial arts schools

PAGE ONE HUNDRED AND ELEVEN

No. 211

No. 212

No. 213

No. 214

No. 215   No. 216

No. 217

and works as follows. Take a right punch with your right palm, Photo No. 216 and step in very close to his body placing your right leg behind his. Your right arm is used across his neck to throw him over your right leg. Photo No. 217.

THANKS TO

LES ANWYL FOR APPEARING IN THE PHOTOS, AN EXCELLENT STUDENT AND FRIEND

PA-KUA CHANG

CHAPTER SEVEN

The internal martial art of PA-KUA CHANG tends to compliment t'ai chi. It is said that t'ai chi is the mother while pa-kua is the daughter. At an advanced level, there is not much difference in the fighting side of pa-kua and t'ai chi so I try to use techniques from both arts in our Chinese Boxing Classes. To this end I have devised certain training techniques that make use of both arts.

The main difference between the two arts in a combat sense is that t'ai chi tends to evade or yeild, blocking the outer lines of defence to attack the centre line. In pa-kua we tend to break anything that comes in contact with the 'hammer palm feelers' and then attack the centre. The both ways of fighting are correct and will of course depend greatly upon the type of body using them. A small person would not try to barge in and break anything that came in contact with his palm but rather evade and attack the centre. The larger person would be able to break anything that came in contact with his palms and then get at the centre. By the same token, a smaller person would usually try to block onto the 'closed side' (covered earlier) to avoid the opponent's other arm or leg. The larger person would not worry so much about the closed side but rather come straight in on either side, crushing everything in his path.

The single pounding palm from pa-kua chang is a most formidable weapon and when used correctly can break an attacking arm or wrist with one blow. The low double handed block from t'ai chi however is used to block very heavy punches or kicks using the both arms and then re-attack very quickly. I have put these two techniques together into a two person training set. This way everyone regardless of size is able to pactise and use both of the above methods and gain something from them.

It has been my experience to know that you will need some form of forearm protection as the pa-kua palm is very powerful.

THE METHOD

Two players stand opposite each other, one the attacker, the other the defender. The defender stands in a PA-KUA slightly side on stance using two No. 3 palms (fire). The palms are medium tense with the rest of the arm and whole body relaxed. The palm should not be so tense that the forearm is also greatly tensed and it should be slightly concaved. The striking portions of the pa-kua palm for this exercise are the harder mount areas starting from below the thumb around the bottom of the palm and up to the knife edge of the palm. The defender's left palm is placed near his own right elbow and is only used as back-up in the first part of the exercise.

The attacker strikes the defender with a right fist to the face while the defender pounds that wrist over to his left with his right thumb mount. Photo No. 118. Note that the palm does not turn, it just stays there like a hammer. Now the attacker throws a left face punch to which the defender answers by pounding it over to his right using the knife edge of his right palm. Photo No. 119. Next the attacker throws a low right punch to the lower left rib area. The defender now relaxes his both palms (in order to use a t'ai chi technique) and using the harder area of his right forearm, blocks it over to his left with the left palm on the top to trap the attacking arm, (or leg). Photo No. 120. Now instantly, the defender controls the attacker's right wrist with his left palm while he uses back-fist to the face. Photo No. 121. This whole set is practised on both sides. There should be minimal time between the low block and the back-fist.

It is said of the single pounding palm in pa-kua that one should be able to block anything that comes within range and immobilise it using only one palm. The other palm is only used if necessary. The t'ai chi low block is an excellent block used for heavy attacks by foot or fist. Practise this method until you are able to reach a reasonable speed with great power in the attacker's attacks.

PAGE ONE HUNDRED AND FIFTEEN

No. 218

No. 219

No. 220

No. 221

Conclusion

I have covered in this book only a small part of one's t'ai chi training. Keep in mind that if the martial art is performed correctly, then the healing art will also work. The main area of training in the internal martial arts is the mind or rather 'no mind.'

If you work with this in mind you will most certainly gain. You may not become the world's greatest fighter or the world's greatest healer, this is not important. Even if you only ever gain one tenth of what t'ai chi has to offer then you will be miles ahead from where you were before. Your daily life will improve as will your work place and your love life etc. You will become a better person. If you <u>are</u> ever attacked physically you will also know how to look after yourself with the least amount of violence and we all of us can do with a little less of that in our lives.

Don't expect what you have learnt in this book to work miracles in about one week. It takes ages for all that I have covered to become sub-conscious. Most of all you need someone with whom to practise. Preferably someone with whom you share your life, then this great art will become a part of your family and your life.

GO TO WORK FOR NUCLEAR DISARMAMENT

GOOD LUCK AND GREAT HAPPINESS BE WITH YOU

ACKNOWLEDGEMENT

AUSTRALASIAN FIGHTING ARTS

The publisher wishes to thank the Martial Arts Magazine "Australasian Fighting Arts" for it's work in promoting all martial arts, Australian and World wide. Address: P/O Box 673 MANLY N.S.W. 2095 AUSTRALIA.

"T'AI CHI" NEWSLETTER

This Magazine has helped more than any other to spread the good word about t'ai chi with articles from all styles and masters from around the world.

P/O Box 26156 Los Angeles CA. 90026 U.S.A.

MARTIAL ARTS WORLD

Martial Arts World is Australias largest Martial Arts Shop, for it's continued assistance in promoting all martial arts.
P/O Box 198F GLADESVILLE N.S.W. 2111 AUSTRALIA.

ST. JAMES HEALTH CARE

Chris And Gina Madden have worked to heal many of my students, sometimes working miracles in acupuncture and ostepathy.
Phone Sydney 02-2671158 or write to the Publisher.

T'AI CHI SECRETS

So you've been with your teacher for fifteen years and you're now asking, what comes next? You wait and wait and eventually, if you've got any brain at all, you'll be thinking that your instructor is keeping things from you. And the answer is that he probably is! This seems to be especially so when we are talking about the Chinese Masters in China or Hong Kong etc. Sure many of these direct lineage masters know the secret techniques but they're not telling. And when they do, it's usually to one of their own family or a very close Chinese student.

There is more and when you learn about it, it's a real eye opener. Why do you suppose that T'ai Chi Ch'uan means 'The Supreme Ultimate Boxing?' To discover the reason we must go right back to when T'ai Chi was invented by Chang San-feng around the beginning of the 13th century. Chang was a famous acupuncturist and was already good at the harder Shaolin styles. But still Chang was not sure that he had the best fighting system in China. So he and two others, also acupuncturists set about the find out what points on the human body would cause which reactions. They knew that certain points would cause either damage or heal from performing acupuncture. Without going into exactly how they worked on the points, after some years the three finally worked out what points and in what combinations, what direction and how hard to strike would cause either death or immobilize an opponent. Then, Chang became quite paranoid in that he did not want anyone else other than his own, to have his discoveries. So he had to have a way in which he could teach his own family and students without letting anyone else find out what it was he was practicing. This form of movement which was really a hidden set of movements, eventually became known as T'ai Chi Ch'uan. But by the time that it was called this, not many people knew why they were doing these movements! The original meaning were lost and only the family members had the good oil. Right up to our present day, this knowledge has only been passed down to a few instructors.

Chang Yiu-chun was one of my instructors and Chang knew the dim-mak or death point striking of T'ai Chi Ch'uan. Putting this together with my own knowledge of acupuncture and that of many of the world's leading authorities, I have put together what I believe to be the original points from Chang San-feng.

BASIC APPLICATIONS AND, SECRET APPLICATIONS.

Most people know about many of the basic applications from the T'ai Chi forms. For instance many know that the postures from 'double p'eng' through to 'pull back' are to block an oncoming attack, lock the wrist and pull the opponent downward. However, there is a much more sinister application for this and all of the other postures. For instance, when we go into 'double p'eng', we are actually striking to a dim-mak point in the neck called 'stomach 9'. This in itself is a death point and works medically by severely lowering the blood pressure of the body by restricting heart activity through the carotid sinus. When struck with the right amount of force and more importantly, in the correct direction, we have heart stoppage. Now, combine this with the next part of that posture, when we roll the palms over and we continue. The left finger further attack to S.9 while the palm of the right hand attacks to a point known as 'gall bladder 14'. The gall bladder, when it is struck, or any of the major G.B. points, medically also causes knock out to occur by causing the heart to stop. Now, as the person is falling down we further attack to a G.B. point on the side of the rib cage called G.B. 24!

This is how T'ai Chi works in the secret martial arts area and indeed why it is called, 'the supreme ultimate.

Every move you make in your T'ai Chi form is indicative of a very dangerous dim-mak point strike. No matter how insignificant the move, it means something! That is why the movements are there and in the correct direction. We do not have to know the correct direction or pressure because they are all there in our T'ai Chi forms, provided of course that these forms have been learnt correctly and from a competent teacher. For instance, the posture known as 'Step Back And Repulse Monkey' must be performed by the attacking palm in a definite downward strike while the other palm comes slightly across the body and down to the hip. This indicates that the palm on the hip has attacked to important heart and lung points on the forearm while the other attacking palm has attacked to a point called CV 17. This ensures that the direction of the strike is going against the flow of energy or qi. Sometimes we just move one palm half an inch but this too has a reason. This is to attack the flow of energy to other parts of the body so that certain limbs will become weakened to a more devastating kick or punch.

THE EYES AND SPACE

Most martial arts tell us something about how we should emulate the actions of animals. We should move like the spritely monkey or pounce like the tiger etc. But the most important of these is that we should have the eye of the eagle ready to strike. When we read this, we usually oversimplify it and just look harder or focus harder. But upon looking further into the Chinese way of the animals in kung-fu we see that the eagle has an unique seeing system which tells us exactly how we should be seeing when fighting.

The eagle has a way of literally locking onto his prey, not just the shape but the space that surrounds it.

We have three visions; spot focus, where we look directly at a smaller portion and focus upon it, average focus, where we use our total peripheral vision to see the whole subject and surrounding area, and small peripheral focus, where we lock onto the space that the object takes up in the universe. This is a very special technique and requires many hours of practice combined with breathing techniques.

In this way we are able to move with the opponent and not wait until he has moved. In other words, we do not see a series of 'pictures' as he moves closer and focus separately on to these images. But rather our sight moves as he moves and follow the space that he displaces. A body can only take up the same amount of space no matter what it is doing and in what shape so if we fight the space displacement then we cannot fail, we move when it moves because we are locked onto that space and so we adjust our own space accordingly and sub-consciously make the right moves to counter.

ON VIDEO

Moon Ta-Gu Books and Erle Montaigue have a video covering all of the above advanced techniques including the fourth level of both forms of Yang and the dim-mak applications from both of these forms.

WRITE FOR A FREE CATTLEDOG: